W9-AVT-073

"A timely and important guide for the practicing clinician. Domestic violence is a silent epidemic that requires sensitivity and skill in recognition and treatment."

—David Lawrence, M.D., Chief Executive Officer
Kaiser Foundation Health Plan, Inc.

"This is the handbook every clinician needs to understand the shocking facts about domestic violence, how to recognize it and deal with it effectively.

Highly recommended for its analysis of the psychology of domestic violence and its practical guidelines for dealing with the problem in a health care setting."

—Sadja Greenwood, M.D., author
Menopause, Naturally: *Preparing for the Second Half of Life*

"An important resource for the medical community!"

—Donna Garske
Marin Abused Women Services

"An excellent guide for physicians to help combat the problem of domestic violence. Full of concrete techniques that medical personnel can use in identifying and responding to domestic violence in medical settings. A must-have for all medical personnel."

—Daniel J. Sonkin, Ph.D., co-author **Learning to Live Without Violence:** *A Handbook for Men*

THE
PHYSICIAN'S GUIDE
TO
DOMESTIC VIOLENCE

How to Ask the Right Questions
and Recognize Abuse
. . . another way to save a life

**Patricia R. Salber, M.D.
and
Ellen Taliaferro, M.D.**

Volcano, California

Library of Congress Cataloging in Publication Data

Salber, Patricia R., 1940–
    Physician's guide to domestic violence: how to ask
    the right questions and recognize abuse, by Patricia R.
    Salber and Ellen Taliaferro.
        p.   cm.
    Includes bibliographical references.
    ISBN 1-884244-04-1
    1. Family violence. 2. Medical emergencies. I.
    Taliaferro, Ellen. II. Title.
        [DNLM: 1. Domestic Violence — prevention &
    control. 2. Physician's Role. W 860 T146p 1994]
    RC569.5.F3T35 1994
    616.85'822 — dc20
    DNLM/DLC
    for Library of Congress
                                         94-23000
                                             CIP

Edited by Zoe Brown
Text and Cover Design by David Charlsen
Composition by Jeff Brandenburg, ImageComp

Please enclose $10.95 for each copy of **THE PHYSICIAN'S
GUIDE TO DOMESTIC VIOLENCE** ordered. For postage and
handling, add $4.50 for the first book and $1.00 for each
additional book. California residents only add appropriate
sales tax. Contact Volcano Press for quantity discount rates
and for a free current catalog.

Volcano Press, Inc.   P.O. Box 270, Volcano CA 95689
     1-800-879-9636   FAX: (209) 296-4515

Printed in the United States of America.

American Medical Association

Physicians dedicated to the health of America

Robert E. McAfee, MD   515 North State Street   312 464-4466
President   Chicago, Illinois 60610   312 464-5543 Fax

November 17, 1994

Ms. Ruth Gottstein, Publisher
Volcano Press
Dear Ms. Gottstein:

I have thoroughly enjoyed reading the first proof of *The Physician's Guide to Domestic Violence*. Please congratulate both Drs. Taliaferro and Salber for their marvelous addition to the armamentarium available to physicians in this country.

"If as a physician, you treat adult patients, then there has been at least one victim of domestic violence in your office in the past two weeks. Who was it? How do you decide? How can you be a better diagnostician? And, more importantly, how can you begin to assist those patients for what happens to be one of the biggest public health problems of our country? How indeed can you, as a physician, break the cycle of violence that exists in many families in this country? Although this violence may be more common in areas of unemployment, inadequate housing and poverty, it nonetheless crosses every socioeconomic category and may be as prevalent in our more affluent society as in the underprivileged. This book fills a definite void in that it is informative, brief, dispels the myths that most of us have about domestic violence and offers guidelines to physicians, both medical and legal, as to what our options are. The dedication of both authors to this cause is quite evident in the plain language and stark reality of the problem as identified in their book. If every physician in this country could have access to this publication, we could indeed make a difference tomorrow in breaking the cycle of violence that is becoming all too common in our society."

Thank you for the opportunity to have reviewed the first proof. I look forward to its final publication. Let me know if I can be of any further assistance to you.

Yours Truly,

Robert E. McAfee, MD
President, American Medical Association

ACKNOWLEDGMENTS

We acknowledge and are thankful for the advice, counsel and support of our teachers and colleagues. Specifically, we would like to thank the entire staff of the Family Violence Prevention Fund, particularly Debbie Lee, Janet Nudleman, and Esta Soler for educating us about domestic violence. They gently, but persistently, reminded us the focus must always be on the needs and wishes of victims, and not on the goals and desires of physicians.

Special thanks are due to the Board of Directors and all of the members of *Physicians for a Violence-free Society* for their support, especially PVS Vice-President Charles Clemons, M.D. who contributed greatly to our understanding of the use and abuse of power in intimate relationships. Thanks also to our colleagues at the Pacific Center for Violence Prevention Liz McLoughlin, Andrew and Kae McGuire, and Robin Trembly-McGaw for their advice, support, and friendship.

We would also like to thank Phil Lee, M.D., Hal Luft, Ph.D. and Drummond Rennie, M.D. and our other teachers at the Institute for Health Policy Studies at the University of California where we completed our Pew Fellowships in Health Policy. They gave us the tools to explore the impact of policy decisions on the lives of patients and the practices of physicians. Some of the suggestions in the last chapter of this book are a direct result of our experiences at the Institute.

Finally we would like to thank all of the individuals who took time out of their busy lives to review and give helpful comments on the manuscript, including Kathleen Delaney, M.D., Bobbie Fisher, Donna Garske, Debbie Lee, Marjorie Little, Carolyn Sachs, M.D., and the staff of the Family Place of Dallas.

CONTENTS

PREFACE

Since early January, 1993, when we co-founded *Physicians for a Violence-free Society* (PVS), we have been heartened by the sincere effort many of our colleagues are making to address domestic violence. It is our belief that the healing professions must be intensely involved in the recognition, intervention, and prevention of domestic violence. Every physician, every healthcare provider can make a difference. The following excerpt from a letter written by Dr. Joseph Sachs, an emergency physician affiliated with the University of California Los Angeles, illustrates this point:

> "At the conclusion of the PVS conference in San Francisco, I had mixed emotions. On the one hand, I felt inspired by the incredible energy and commitment of the PVS members and leadership. On the other hand, I had some serious doubt . . . Can a group of doctors really make a difference?
>
> The day after the conference, I returned to my duties in the Emergency Department . . . a second-year resident presented the case of a thirty-year-old woman with chest pain. As a teacher, I feel obliged to offer up a few pearls of wisdom . . . filled with new knowledge from the PVS conference, I decided to enlighten the resident about the problem of domestic violence. What happened next was nothing short of a miracle. After two simple questions about domestic violence, the woman broke into tears. Her husband had been beating her for the past fourteen years, but she had been too afraid to tell anyone. Further questioning revealed that the husband also routinely beat her three children with a baseball bat.

Before the PVS conference, this woman would have been discharged with a prescription for ibuprofen. Instead, she received supportive counseling and was referred to a shelter. Her children were placed in a safe foster home while the police and children's service personnel began their investigation.

I'll admit that I was initially skeptical about the impact and the effectiveness of the PVS conference. But on the very next day, we saved four lives. All because of what I learned in San Francisco.

Let us be inspired and committed to educate our medical students, residents, colleagues, and patients about issues of violence and violence prevention. Believe me, we can make a tremendous difference."

The mere fact that you have begun to read this book identifies you as a concerned and committed caregiver who truly wishes to make a difference in this area.

We have specifically designed this handbook to be an easy to read, user-friendly "how to" manual for busy physicians. It gives an overview of domestic violence as well as practical advice on how to begin incorporating domestic violence intervention and prevention into your practice. To accomplish the aims of this book, we have abandoned formal academic writing and adopted a more informal and conversational style. For rapid access to the information, we have listed topics within the chapters on the contents page.

We sincerely hope this book will help you acquire the knowledge and skills essential for effective intervention in domestic violence.

Patricia R. Salber, M.D.
Ellen Taliaferro, M.D.

Chapter One

AN INTRODUCTION TO DOMESTIC VIOLENCE

Domestic violence affects millions of people each year. In the United States, two to four million women are battered annually by their intimate partners. Although physical abuse may be limited to a single individual, all family members who witness the abuse suffer as well. Home for these families is not a safe haven, but a place where violence can erupt at any time.

The effects of domestic violence are far-reaching, affecting not only families but also communities, institutions, and society as a whole. It adversely impacts the criminal justice system, social services, the legal system, the educational system and the workplace. It also has significant effects on the health-care system.

Abused women and their children are our patients. So are the batterers. We treat injuries and illness — both physical and mental — directly related to the violence in their lives. Many victims are seen repeatedly before the domestic abuse is discovered. In some instances, the violence is never identified, and the physician continues to work up myriad complaints without making a definitive diagnosis. This adds to the high dollar cost of providing medical care to victims. And it prolongs the agony for families trapped in a repetitive cycle of violence.

For the health and safety of our patients and their families, it is imperative that we acquire the knowledge and skills to identify and respond appropriately to this pervasive problem.

Some Definitions

Family violence as a term encompasses all violence that occurs inside a family unit. It is an umbrella term which includes partner, child, sibling, parent, and elder abuse. *Domestic violence* is the term used to denote violence which one adult (or adolescent) intimate inflicts on another. Other terms used for this type of violence are *partner abuse, spouse abuse, woman abuse* and *wife-beating.**

There are limitations to all of these terms. Domestic violence implies that violence occurs in the home; how-

---

* In this book, the male pronoun "he" is used when referring to perpetrators of domestic violence; victims are referred to as "she." This is because most batterers are men and most battering victims are women.

ever, a great number of women are no longer living with the men who abuse them — they are really ex-partners or ex-spouses. Of course, the terms woman abuse and wife-beating are not useful to describe domestic violence that occurs in gay male or lesbian relationships, or in the uncommon situation where a female batters her male partner.

Power and Control

Domestic violence is not just about hitting or punching. Rather, it is a pattern of assaultive and coercive behaviors, including psychological, sexual, and physical abuse, used by an individual to hurt, dominate, and control an intimate partner. Table 1 lists examples of tactics used by these individuals to gain power in order to control their partners.

Without intervention, the abuse is usually recurrent and can escalate in frequency and severity. The syndrome of dominance and control by the perpetrator leading to increasing entrapment of the victim is also known as the *battering syndrome.*

TABLE 1. TACTICS USED BY BATTERERS TO GAIN POWER AND CONTROL OVER THEIR PARTNERS

CATEGORY	EXAMPLE
Verbal abuse	"You're stupid. It's a good thing I am here to take care of you."
Emotional abuse	A victim may be coerced into doing humiliating things (such as waiting in the car while her partner visits his mistress) or she may be forced to do things against her religious or moral principles (such as telling lies or stealing)
Using children	He threatens or actually takes the children away to force the victim to do what he wants.
Isolation	The victim is cut off from friends and family. There is no one she can talk to about the abuse.
Use of "male privilege"	"It's the man's right to choose where we live and how we live."
Economic abuse	All of the family's finances are controlled by the batterer. She has no independent access to any money.
Threats of or actual physical abuse of children or pets or destruction of property	"If you leave me, I will harm the children."
Sexual abuse	Sexual abuse (partner rape) occurs in many violent relationships
Threats of physical abuse	"I will kill you if you leave me."
Physical abuse	Pushing, punching, slapping, throwing, choking, stabbing, shooting, etc.

A Brief History

Until recently, wife-beating was an accepted part of marriage in many cultures. Women were considered the property of men and were subject to a variety of abuses, including physical punishment for their "misbehaviors." British common law allowed men to "chastise" their wives with "any reasonable instrument." It was eventually modified to state that the weapon used to beat her must be no thicker than his thumb — thus we have the term "the rule of thumb." This rule was instituted to protect women, but underscored the societal belief that it was a woman's lot to be beaten into submission if she did not mind her husband.

In the United States, it wasn't until 1895 that the Married Women's Property Act gave women the right to use conviction for assault as sufficient grounds for divorce. However, as recently as 1962 a woman in California who wanted to sue her husband for assault was turned down by the judge because, "the case would destroy the peace and harmony of the home, and thus would be contrary to the policy of the law."[*]

The battered women's movement, which spearheaded the development and proliferation of shelters for battered women, had its roots in the women's movement of the late 1960s and early 1970s. A National Coalition Against Domestic Violence was formed in 1978. Today there are over twelve hundred shelters in this country.

---

[*] G. NiCarthy, *Getting Free: You Can End Abuse and Take Back Your Life.* Washington: The Seal Press. 1986. Pg 4.

The first model programs for addressing domestic violence in the health-care setting began to appear in the 1980s. In 1985, Surgeon General C. Everett Koop declared domestic violence to be a public health problem. The Joint Commission on Accreditation of Healthcare Organizations approved the adoption of new standards relating to the identification, evaluation, and provision of care to adult victims of domestic violence. These standards went into effect in January 1992. In March of the same year, the American Medical Association published their *Diagnostic and Treatment Guidelines on Domestic Violence* and launched a national campaign against domestic violence.

A National Center for Injury Prevention and Control was established at the Centers for Disease Control and Prevention in Atlanta in June of 1992. The prevention of violence against women is an important part of the agenda for the center. The goals of this agency are:

1. To institute a surveillance system in order to gather information about how often domestic violence occurs, risk factors, and trends,
2. To demonstrate and evaluate ways to prevent violence against women,
3. To conduct a national communications effort to help people recognize that violence against women is unacceptable and preventable,
4. To develop a national network of organizations and coalitions to support state and local health department efforts to prevent violence against women, and

5. To increase knowledge of modifiable factors associated with violence against women and to develop new prevention strategies based on that knowledge.

Proposals for projects in the area of domestic violence have already been developed and funded.

Until very recently, few medical schools included domestic violence — adult partner abuse — in their curricula. Residency programs, even in specialties seeing large numbers of battered women, did not have formal training in the recognition and referral of victims of domestic abuse.

Today, more and more medical schools are recognizing domestic violence in their programs. Curricular principles taking note of family violence have been developed by a group of experts meeting at the 1994 Family Violence and Health Professions Education Conference held in Oklahoma City. Hopefully these will eventually be adopted by medical schools across the country. Residency programs in such specialties as Obstetrics and Gynecology and Emergency Medicine are formally teaching their residents about domestic violence. Chapters on this subject are starting to appear in general and specialty medical textbooks.

Finally, practicing physicians are seeking more information about how to appropriately screen, identify, and refer victims of domestic violence. We hope this text will be helpful in this regard.

Magnitude of the Problem

It is important to point out that estimates of the number of battered women vary widely in both the popular and medical literature. Sources of these statistics include state and local surveys, the National Crime Survey and local, state, and national police reports. These instruments are believed to underestimate the true incidence of domestic violence. Many victims fail to report battering to the police due to shame or because of fear of further violent repercussions. Death reports provide another source of information on domestic violence, however, these only capture one subset of victims, those with a fatal outcome.

Despite the difficulties with reported statistics, it is nevertheless clear that domestic violence is a huge problem in this country. Conservative studies indicate that nearly twelve million women in the United States will be abused at some time during their lives. Many of these women will be beaten repeatedly. Almost half of the men who beat their partners do so three or more times a year. Rape is a significant form of abuse, occurring in many violent relationships. Domestic violence can be fatal — approximately fifteen hundred to two thousand women are killed by their partners or ex-partners each year.

The Effect of Domestic Violence on the Medical System

Reviews of domestic violence in the medical literature often report incidence or prevalence figures which were extrapolated from small studies carried out in restricted settings — for example, retrospective chart reviews of injured women in an inner city trauma center or a survey of women seeking care in one ambulatory care clinic of a tertiary care hospital. Despite the methodological difficulties of such data, it is nonetheless clear that domestic violence has a large impact on the healthcare system.

TABLE 2. DATA REPORTED IN VARIOUS STUDIES ON THE INCIDENCE AND PREVALENCE OF DOMESTIC VIOLENCE

- The American Medical Association has estimated that 28 percent of women seen in ambulatory clinics have been battered at some time during their lives; 14 percent are currently battered.
- About 20-25 percent of pregnant women seeking prenatal care are in battering relationships.
- Close to 50 percent of mothers of abused children are themselves abused.
- Approximately 10 to 15 percent of women coming to emergency departments with physical injuries are battered.
- Battered women account for 25 percent of women who attempt suicide and 25 percent of women using a psychiatric emergency service.
- One study determined that approximately 63 percent of female psychiatric inpatients had a history of physical abuse, the majority of which was inflicted by adults sharing their homes.

Although family physicians, obstetricians, and emergency physicians are sometimes considered the most likely to see battered women, in fact, physicians of every specialty take care of battered women and/or their children.

TABLE 3. **PRESENTATIONS OF DOMESTIC VIOLENCE TO MEDICAL SPECIALISTS**

- Experts in substance abuse must remember that battering can be the cause of a woman's excessive alcohol or other drug use and that some women become dependent on sedatives and other medications prescribed by their physicians to treat symptoms due to unrecognized domestic abuse.

- Ophthalmologists see battered women with retinal detachments and orbital blow-out fractures.

- Otolaryngologists and maxillofacial surgeons see women with facial lacerations and facial fractures.

Continued on next page

Table 3, continued

- Neurosurgeons become involved when serious head injuries, such as skull fractures, subdural and epidural hematomata, or spinal-cord injuries occur as a result of battering.

- Pediatricians treat battered teens and gerontologists treat battered elders.

- Gastroenterologists see many women with "functional gastrointestinal disorders. Women with these complaints are much more likely than those with an organic disorder to report a history of physical or sexual abuse either as an adult or in childhood.[*]

- There is a significant history of prior or current abuse in women with chronic pelvic pain whose work-up has failed to reveal an organic cause. Gynecologists often see women who fit this description.

- Specialists in rehabilitation treat battered women recovering from a variety of injuries.

- Psychiatrists see acute psychiatric manifestations, such as suicide attempts, as well as more chronic results such as chronic anxiety, depression, and symptoms of post-traumatic stress disorder.

[*] Douglas A. Drossman, et al. "Sexual and physical abuse in women with functional or organic gastrointestinal disorders." *Annals of Internal Medicine* 113:828-833. 1990.

Physicians Often Fail to Recognize Domestic Violence

Despite the prevalence of battered women in the medical setting, studies have documented a failure on the part of physicians to correctly identify and refer abused patients.

- One study found that only 5 percent of 107 victims of domestic violence seen in a metropolitan emergency department were correctly identified as such by physicians on the department's report.[*]

Even if the domestic violence is identified, physicians often fail to respond appropriately. A study of women seriously injured by a partner found that:

- Only one in four times did the physician determine the woman's relationship to her assailant.
- The physician asked about a history of sexual or physical abuse, about the woman's living situation, and performed an assessment of her safety in only 10 percent of cases.
- Psychiatric consultation was obtained in only 4 percent of cases, social service in 8 percent.
- Only 2 percent of women received an information sheet.[**]

---

[*] W. G. Goldberg and M. C. Tomlanovich. "Domestic violence victims in the emergency department." *JAMA*, June 22/29, 1984.
[**] Carole Warshaw. "Limitations of the medical model in the care of battered women." Chicago, Il. *Gender & Society*, December 1989.

There Are Many Reasons Why Physicians Fail to Identify Abuse

To improve our ability to identify domestic violence in our patients, it is important to consider factors that impede diagnosis. For the sake of clarity, the factors will be divided into patient factors, personal (physician factors), and structural factors. Many of these factors may be at play for any given physician-patient interaction.

Patient Factors

Some battered women fail to tell their physicians about the abuse. There are many reasons for this.

TABLE 4. **WHY WOMEN DON'T TELL THEIR DOCTORS ABOUT THE ABUSE**

1. Fear of retribution if the batterer learns the violence has been disclosed:
   - She may not know that what a patient tells her doctor is confidential.
   - She may live in a state with mandatory reporting laws — she fears a police report will trigger an outburst of violence which will endanger her and her family.
   - She may be unable to see her doctor without her batterer being there.
   - Her batterer may have threatened to kill her or their children if she ever told *anyone.*

2. Shame and humiliation that this is happening to her:
   - She may believe she is the only one who lives in this kind of situation.
   - She may believe she caused the violence because she failed her spouse in some way (e.g., didn't clean the house well enough, didn't keep the children quiet, didn't dress the right way, etc.).
   - She may have been told to leave, or she may have tried to leave, and she is ashamed because she is still with her batterer.

3. She may think she deserved the abuse:
   - She thinks she doesn't deserve to be helped.

4. She may feel protective of her partner:
   - He is her main source of love and affection when he is not being abusive.

Continued on next page

Table 4, continued

- He is her and her children's sole support.
- She hopes he will change.

5. She may not fully comprehend her situation:

   - She believes all marriages have "fights" like theirs.
   - She believes the violence won't occur again.
   - She may not be aware that her physical symptoms are related to the stress of living in an abusive situation.
   - She may think the injuries she has sustained are not severe enough to mention.
   - Her cultural, ethnic, and/or religious background influences her response to the abuse.

6. She may think her doctor is not knowledgeable or does not care about domestic violence. Or she may think her doctor is too busy to spend time talking about this problem.

   - On her last clinic visit, she tried to tell her doctor she was nervous because of stress at home. Without asking about the cause of the stress, the doctor quickly wrote a prescription for an anxiolytic and left abruptly to see the next patient.

7. She may think her doctor couldn't help her with this problem.

   - She does not know that physicians can provide her with the information she needs in order to do something about her situation.
   - She may have told a physician in the past and got no response.

Personal (Physician) Factors

A recent study of California emergency departments[*] revealed that emergency physicians and nurses felt the most significant barriers to identification of domestic violence resided in the patient — she did not voluntarily reveal, or may have denied, domestic violence during the ED visit. This result is interesting in the face of reports in the medical literature that battered women expect doctors to ask about abuse and will respond when asked in an empathetic and nonjudgmental manner.

Why don't doctors routinely inquire about domestic violence as a primary or contributing cause of their patients presenting complaints or past medical problems? One study demonstrated clearly that physicians' own beliefs and motivations play a major role.[**] Thirty-eight primary-care physicians were queried to determine their perceptions of barriers to recognition and intervention of domestic violence in their practice.

- Eighteen percent of the physicians used the phrase "opening Pandora's box" to describe their reactions to exploring the issue of domestic violence with their patients. (Pandora, according to Greek mythology, was created by Zeus in revenge for Prometheus' providing mankind with fire. Pandora opened a box out of which flew labor, aging, sickness, insanity, passion, and vice.)

---

[*] Debbie Lee, et al. *The Impact of Domestic Violence on the Emergency Department.* California Hospital Emergency Departments. 1993.
[**] N. K. Sugg & T. Inui. "Primary care physicians' response to domestic violence." *JAMA.* June 17, 1992.

- Eight percent used phrases such as "opening a can of worms."
- Physicians' close identification with patients was an inhibitory factor in 39 percent of physicians interviewed. For example, doctors from white, middle-class backgrounds who had no experience with domestic violence assumed that their patients with similar backgrounds would not be involved in situations of domestic abuse.
- Women physicians who closely identified with their patients were subject to another factor: The discovery of domestic violence in patients similar to themselves could expose their own fear of vulnerability and lack of control.

On the other hand, the feeling of being "too close for comfort" may exist because the physician is or has been a victim or a perpetrator of domestic violence. Asking patients about domestic violence might mean they would have to confront the violence in their own lives. Although attitudes have been changing over the last two decades, societal beliefs about male superiority and female submission persist. Some physicians of both sexes share these beliefs, and this can affect their ability to effectively identify and intervene in cases of domestic violence.

One of the strongest factors inhibiting the exploration of domestic violence is the fear of offending patients. This is followed closely by a sense of powerlessness or the inability to fix it.

Although time constraints were not felt to be a significant barrier to the identification of domestic violence in the California study of emergency departments, other physicians have expressed concern about the amount of time they believe is required to deal with this issue. This concern may be compounded in this era of managed care, with physicians feeling the dual pressures to see more patients per hour and the need to provide comprehensive care. Physicians must be assured that with proper training and skills as well as advance preparation in their practice setting, they can identify, assess, counsel, and refer victims of domestic violence in a reasonable amount of time. Furthermore, they must understand that many domestic violence victims repeatedly access the health-care system before they are identified. Asking directly about violence as a cause or contributing factor to a woman's symptoms may save time and money in the long run.

Other reasons why doctors don't ask about domestic violence are discussed in Table 5.

TABLE 5. **OTHER REASONS PHYSICIANS DON'T ASK ABOUT DOMESTIC VIOLENCE**

1. They believe that domestic violence doesn't occur in the patient population they serve,
   - but domestic violence can happen to anyone, regardless of age, race, socioeconomic status, or educational background (see Chapter 2).

2. The patient is tearful and uncooperative or she is intoxicated from alcohol or other drugs making it difficult to get the history,
   - but we usually don't use these as reasons for missing other potentially fatal conditions.

3. They think the woman provoked or deserved the abuse,
   - but no matter what, no one deserves to be beaten.

4. They believe what happens in the home, in terms of domestic violence, is a private matter and therefore should not be discussed,
   - but physicians routinely ask about other "private matters" that affect their patients' health and well-being, such as sexual preferences and sexual practices.

5. They think she can just leave if she wants to,
   - but there are many reasons why women can't "just leave." These are discussed in more detail in Chapters 2 and 4.

Continued on next page

Table 5, continued

6. They know the assailant and believe he is incapable of abuse,

   • but the outward appearance of many batterers belies their potential for domestic violence.

7. They don't know what to do if they uncover the abuse or they believe it is the job of other professionals, such as social workers,

   • but physicians can play a very important role in identification of the abuse and referral of the patient.

8. They know what to do, but believe it won't help — "she just goes back to him anyway,"

   • but some women do eventually leave — sometimes with the help of their physicians.

Structural Factors

Some hospital settings, especially emergency departments, are not conducive to discussions about domestic violence. The triage or reception area may be semipublic. Patients are asked to explain the reason for their visit while other people are listening or watching. The exam "room" in the ED may only be a space with a gurney which is partitioned from other patients by a flimsy curtain. The same may be true in some clinic settings as well. Lack of privacy can impede a woman's ability to talk about the violence.

In our multicultural society, we often take care of patients who don't speak English. The patient may not disclose the violence when her family members serve as translators. Hospital or clinic translators can be used, but this interferes with the privacy of the doctor-patient relationship. Also, the story may be altered during translation because of the translator's own experiences, perceptions, and prejudices about domestic violence. Finally, the victim or her family may know the translator from other activities in their community, thus making her reluctant to disclose the abuse.

Doing It Right

Physicians can acquire the knowledge and skills to intervene effectively in domestic violence. The study discussed earlier, on physicians' attitudes about asking about domestic violence, described two physicians who were, in fact, "doing it right."

- One had a previous history of abuse and had received counseling.
- The other had encountered several cases of domestic violence in the early days of his practice. He had experienced positive outcomes with these patients, and his subsequent reading and study in this area had left him with a sense of competency in dealing with these issues.

What both of these physicians exhibited in addressing this issue was a sense of competency and comfort. This was reflected in their practice.

Chapter Two

WHAT DO WE KNOW ABOUT THE VICTIMS OF DOMESTIC VIOLENCE?

There are many misconceptions about who is likely to become a victim of domestic violence. Most people believe it could never happen to anyone like themselves. However, any woman can become a victim — regardless of race, ethnicity, age, socioeconomic or educational status. There are no *typical* victims.

Gender

Various studies show that victims of domestic violence are predominantly women.

- According to the crime reports, most reported victims are women and most reported perpetrators are men.

- Although some studies have shown American men and women to be at similar risk for experiencing partner assault (approximately 30-40 episodes of severe violence/1000 individuals), physical abuse of men by women often occurs after the man initiates the violence and the women uses force to protect herself.

- Furthermore, women are 13 times more likely than men to be *injured* by partner violence.[*] Domestic violence is a pattern of controlling behaviors aimed at gaining power in order to control an intimate partner. Assault without actual or realistic threat of injury does not have the same controlling effect on the partner as assault where injury is likely.

- Women are 1.3 times more likely to be killed by their spouse than men.[**] Women who kill their husbands usually do so after a long and severe history of battering. Angela Browne[***] compared the characteristics of battered women who killed their partners with those who did not. The only difference was that the spouses of women who killed were more violent than those of women who did not. The fact that 70 percent of spouse homicides involve the use of firearms may account for the less dramatic difference between male and female homicide rates compared to injury rates.

[*] Stark Flitcraft. "Spouse abuse" in *Violence in America*. New York, N.Y. Oxford University Press. 1991.
[**] J. A. Mercy & L. E. Saltzman. "Fatal violence among spouses in the United States, 1976–85." *AJPH*. May 1989.
[***] A. Browne. *When Battered Women Kill*. New York, N.Y., Macmillan/Free Press. 1987.

- The syndrome of entrapment, known as the battering syndrome, has so far only been identified as a problem for women.

Ethnic and Socioeconomic Considerations

Partner abuse — physical and sexual — occurs in all ethnic and socioeconomic groups.

- African-American women are more likely than white women to report domestic violence to the authorities. They are also more likely than white women to seek medical care because of battering.
- Although occupational class is not related to domestic violence, social status inconsistency (for example, the female partner is in a higher or lower class or job status than the man) has been reported to increase a woman's risk of being victimized.
- Studies on attitudes of physicians towards child abuse suggest that physicians *may be more likely to diagnose abuse* in poor patients and/or those from ethnic minorities.
- Interracial marriages and mixed religion marriages appear to be at higher risk than marriages without such differences.

Age

Domestic violence is more common among couples under thirty, possibly because violent relationships may be more likely to end early due to separation, divorce, or death. Domestic violence, however, can occur at any age.

- Approximately half of elder abuse is actually partner abuse in older couples.

An eighty-six-year-old woman was taken to the Emergency Department after developing confusion and garbled speech. A CT scan revealed a large subdural hematoma with a shift of the midline. She died a short time later. A coroner's investigation revealed other injuries, both new and old, suggestive of spousal abuse. Her eighty-eight-year-old husband was named as the prime suspect in the case.

- Abuse occurs between teen-aged and other young dating couples.

According to the Adolescent Violence Prevention Resource Center,

- Approximately one out of ten high school students experiences physical violence in a dating relationship.
- More than 70 percent of pregnant or parenting teens are beaten by their boyfriends.
- Date rape accounts for 60 percent of all reported rapes; the majority of date rape victims are between the ages of sixteen and twenty-four.

Marriages in which there is a disparity of age between the couples may be at higher risk than marriages without such differences.

Marital Status
Single, separated, and divorced women may be more likely than married women to experience assault by a male intimate. It is important to recognize that separation or divorce may increase a woman's risk of serious injury or death due to abuse. This can play a role in a woman's reluctance to leave the relationship.

Personality Traits
Early studies suggested that women with certain personality traits, such as poor self-esteem, were more likely to become battered. Subsequent research has failed to support this and no consistent personality profile has been identified for battered women.[*]

Pregnancy
Pregnancy can be an especially high-risk time for some abused women. It has been reported that somewhere between 20 and 25 percent of all obstetrical patients are in battering relationships.

- Battering can begin or escalate during pregnancy
- The pattern of the abuse also may change from injuries to the head and neck to injuries on the breasts and abdomen.

---

[*] G. T. Hotaling and D. B. Sugarman, "An analysis of risk markers in husband to wife violence. The current state of knowledge." *Violence and Victims* 1 (2) 101-124, 1986.

• Battering during pregnancy carries a significant risk of miscarriage or abortion, fetal injury, and poor birth outcome, such as low birthweight.

Sexual Orientation

Very little is known about abuse in same-sex relationships, perhaps in part due to the reluctance of people in the gay community to involve police in their lives. Experts in the field believe that partner abuse probably occurs as least as often in homosexual relationships as in heterosexual relationships. It is interesting to speculate on this supposition in view of the predominance of gender-based theories — such as male dominance — on the cause of domestic violence.

Disabilities

Disabled women are, perhaps, even more vulnerable to abuse by their spouses. They may also be less able to defend themselves. The abusive partner may attempt to control her by keeping her medications from her, destroying prosthetic devices and assistive devices, such as wheelchairs or walkers. She may be dependent on him to keep her medical appointments, provide her with health insurance, and pay the medical bills and costs of living.

Immigration Status

Battered immigrant women, especially undocumented immigrants, are also especially vulnerable to control by their batterers. They may be more easily isolated from the rest of the community because of language barriers. They may fear the police because they are worried their immigration status will be discovered and lead to deportation with loss of contact with their children. They may fear the police because of police brutality in their country of origin. Finally, the batterer may use his victim's immigration status in his threats to report her and have her deported. He may tell her he will keep the children and she will never see them again. For women in these situations, it may really appear that there is no safe option but to submit to abuse.

Use of Alcohol and Drugs
Although clinicians often believe that alcohol and/or drugs are *causative* in both violent acts and victimization, a body of literature exists which suggests that alcohol and drug use in victims may the consequence of the violence and not the cause.

Family History
Early studies suggested that women who grew up in violent homes were at significant risk of becoming victims of violence. Later studies, however, have failed to find a significant effect of childhood violence or prior domestic violence relationships on later victimization.[*]

Understanding Why Victims Don't "Just Leave"
There are many reasons why battered women don't just leave the relationship.

---

[*] L. Walker, *The Battered Woman Syndrome*, New York: Springer. 1984.

TABLE 6. **WHY WOMEN STAY IN ABUSIVE RELATIONSHIPS**

1. One very important reason why women don't leave — or leave and then return to the relationship — is the very real fear of an escalation of the violence when she tries to leave.

   • He has told her he will kill her if she leaves.
   • Or, he hasn't told her explicitly, but she believes from his threats and actions, that he will kill her if she leaves.
   • Research shows that there is an increased risk of serious injury and death at the time battered women leave their partners.
   • He has told her and/or she believes he would harm the children, other family members, friends, or pets if she leaves.

2. There is a lack of real alternatives for housing, employment, and financial assistance.

3. She believes her children need an intact family.

4. She believes she could not provide her children with a decent home, clothing, and schooling.

5. She is immobilized by psychological or physical trauma.

6. She has cultural, religious, or family values that encourage the maintenance of the family unit at all costs.

7. She believes the violence is her fault.

8. She still loves him. She does not want to end the relationship, she just wants the violence to stop.

The Children Are Victims Too

Children are physically abused in about a half of domestic violence cases. Often the child abuse starts after the partner abuse. It may be one more tactic used to control the adult intimate partner. Sometimes children are inadvertently harmed when they attempt to break up fights or to protect their mother.

Even if the children are not physically harmed, witnessing domestic violence has profound effects on them. Research has demonstrated significant emotional, behavioral, and cognitive effects which vary depending on the age at exposure and duration of the violence. Children from violent homes may have difficulties sleeping, eating disorders, depression and neediness, or aggression and rage. They may be seen by pediatricians because of a variety of somatic complaints, fingerbiting, stuttering, or learning difficulties. They may become suicidal. Physical abuse and neglect in childhood may also be associated with behavioral difficulties in adolescence and adulthood. These problems in later life may be as severe as the perpetration of criminal activities, including domestic violence.

Chapter Three

WHAT DO WE KNOW ABOUT THE PERPETRATORS OF DOMESTIC VIOLENCE?

Just as there are no typical victims of domestic violence, there are no typical perpetrators in terms of age, race, socioeconomic status, or other demographic features.

Critical Risk Factors

Although there is inconsistency in the literature on abusers, one risk factor stands out most clearly:

- Having witnessed abuse in the family as a child.

Prior to 1980 when there was almost no empirical literature about male batterers, clinical observations — bolstered by a few national and regional epidemiologic surveys — indicated that men who battered were basically "normal" men who were particularly sexist in their socialization. They tend to have a high need for power and control, lack of assertiveness skills, a tendency to externalize responsibility, denial and minimalization, low self-esteem, and alcohol and drug abuse.

- Typically, as a group, batterers lack assertive interpersonal skills.
- Batterers exhibit difficulty in clearly asking for what they want and in setting expectations for others.
- The male batterer is very likely to externalize responsibility for his violence when it does become known.

"You know, doc, if she wouldn't have come home so late, I wouldn't have had to hit her."

"I had a big project due at work and she just wouldn't leave me alone."

Although most batterers may not have a diagnosable personality problem, there is a subset of battering men who have a variety of personality disorders or psycho-pathology such as:

- borderline personality
- narcissistic personality
- antisocial personality
- passive-dependent personality
- passive-aggressive personality

Dominance of Men over Women

Many experts hold that domestic violence is rooted in a cultural and societal belief in the dominance of men over women. According to this belief, men are allowed to control women using any means, including violence.

Men Choose to Be Violent

It is not uncommon to hear or read that a perpetrator battered his spouse because he was in a "blind rage" or the act was justified because it was a "crime of passion." Such terminology implies that he really couldn't help himself; he was compelled by forces beyond his control.

Many authorities believe, however, that perpetrators are not out of control and they, in fact, choose to be violent.

- These men have learned that violence is an effective way to gain control over their partners.
- They have also learned that, by and large, there are very few negative societal consequences for this behavior.

- They believe they have the right to assume authority over their partner and that it is her role to be subservient to him.

Alcohol and Drugs

Alcohol and drugs do not cause nonviolent people to become violent. There are many perpetrators of domestic violence who neither drink nor use drugs. In addition, some perpetrators abuse their partners whether they are drinking or not. There is evidence however, that drug and alcohol use may be used as an *excuse* for perpetrating the violence.

"I never hit her when I am sober. The alcohol just has that effect on me."

"Snorting coke just makes me crazy."

Although drug and alcohol use do not cause violence, their use may increase the risk of violence in some situations and is relevant when assessing potential lethality and planning for the safety of the victim (see pages 61–65).

Secrecy and Denial

Perpetrators share the use of secrecy, denial, blame, collusion, and minimization.

- The perpetrator will often go to great lengths to hide the fact of his violence from the outside world.
- When that fails and he is confronted, he will often deny the violence has occurred. To do this he may have to attack the credibility of the victim and others who accuse him. He will say the event never happened or that the victim (or other accuser) lies or is prone to exaggeration.
- If that fails, he will say the victim precipitated the violence or brought it on herself.
- He may get "others" (family, friends, co-workers) to support him against her.
- Finally, he may say, "Yes, it did happen, but that was in the past. It is time to forgive and forget and get on with life."

Common to these approaches is the perpetrator's refusal to accept responsibility for his actions. When those of us in the health-care system ignore the abuse, we reinforce his view that the violence is acceptable.

Chapter Four

POWER AND CONTROL

As discussed in the first chapter, domestic violence is not defined simply by physical acts of hitting, slapping or punching in a relationship, but also by the use of a variety of tactics, including physical assault, by one intimate with the goal of gaining power and control over his partner. Domestic violence is about *power and control.*

Tactics used by batterers to gain power and control over their victims range from verbal abuse to physical violence. (See Table 1 in Chapter 1.)

Verbal Abuse

Victims of domestic violence frequently describe verbal abuse as a prominent feature in their relationship with their batterer. They are told they are stupid or crazy or incompetent; they could not possibly survive in the world without the batterer's help. They are called belittling names, such as "lard-butt" or "airhead;" nothing they do is ever done right. The verbal abuse may have more than one purpose — it destroys her self-confidence, raises his stature, and controls her behavior. For example, one woman who had been abused for ten years was repeatedly told by her husband that no one would believe her if she ever talked about the abuse because she was "just an alcoholic" and he, on the other hand, was a respected attorney.

Emotional Abuse

Emotional abuse can take many forms. It can be repeated verbal attacks as discussed above. Or it may consist of the batterer coercing her into doing things she finds humiliating, such as watching while her partner makes love to his mistress or cleaning up food which he has deliberately thrown on the floor in front of guests. It may involve forcing her to do things which are against her moral or religious principles, such as lying or stealing. The batterer may direct her to do things or behave in a certain way and then deny later that he asked her to do it. All of these tactics have a common purpose — to maintain authority over the victim.

Isolation

Victims of domestic violence are often isolated from their families and friends. Batterers find fault with the victims social contacts and raise objections to her continued relationship with them. The objections may be couched in terms of sexual jealousy ("I know you are having an affair with John — that's why you stay late at the office"). Or, they may be insults or put-downs of the individuals. ("How can you waste your time with Jane?

I don't like her. She is so dumb. Anyone who hangs around with her must be stupid too.") Attempts to defend these relationships may serve as focal points for arguments. Victims describe cutting off relationships with families and friends in order to avoid outbursts of violent behavior on the part of the batterer.

Isolation in some cases includes a physical shutting off of the victim from the outside world. Telephones may be ripped from the wall, TV sets and radios smashed, and newspaper service canceled. Some women describe being locked inside the house or even a closet when their batterer goes to work. In these cases the batterer becomes the victim's sole contact with the outside world — he defines her reality.

In some cases, victims contribute to their isolation. They cancel appointments, miss work, and stay at home to hide a black eye or a broken tooth or to avoid angering their partner. Breaking off from a best friend allows a woman to avoid the questioning looks or lectures about why she should leave her batterer. It also helps avoid her partner's using the friendship as a reason to perpetrate violence.

Use of Children

The batterer may threaten to take the children from the victim if she does not behave the way he wants. He threatens or actually abuses them in order to gain control over her. He makes them watch as he abuses her or he forces them to participate in the abuse. He insists the children spy on her and tell him about her every activity. If she leaves, he continues to use the fear of losing the children as a means of controlling her, either by long, expensive child custody battles or by threats or actual kidnapping of them. Court-ordered visitations are used to control her behavior as he determines when and where they take place. She knows she is at risk during the time she has to take the children to him.

> Sharon arranged to meet her ex-husband in the parking lot of a busy shopping mall, close to the local police station. She believed this would keep her safe when she had to bring the children for their court-mandated visit with him. While she was bending over to get her youngest out of the car seat, he grabbed her from behind, slit her throat, and stabbed her a number of times in the abdomen.

Use of "Male Privilege"

Gender role stereotypes play a dominant role in battering relationships. There are responsibilities and privileges tied to the sex of the partner. For example, cooking may be her job and mowing the lawn his job. It used to be a tradition for men to open the door to the car or walk on the outside of the sidewalk. These were, and in some places and relationships continue to be, privileges tied to the female gender. On the other hand, some women always defer to the husband's wishes even when contrary to their own desires because of a belief that this is a part of male privilege. Batterers may take advantage of gender role stereotypes or "male privilege" in order to control their partners. For example, he may force unwanted sex on his wife because of the belief that it is a husband's right to have sexual intercourse with his wife whenever he wants.

Economic Abuse

Victims of domestic violence may have no independent access to money even if they are working. Harassed by the batterer, she may turn over her paycheck as a way of avoiding further abuse. Women who work may find their activities outside of the home a focal point for arguments. Insinuations of impropriety with co-workers and jealousy because of attention paid to others may escalate into full-blown fights. Some women quit their jobs believing this will help stop the violence.

Sexual Abuse

Many women in violent relationships report having been sexually abused. The sexual abuse can take many different forms ranging from coercing sex through verbal threats and physical force (rape). It also includes degrading the woman by coercing or forcing her to have sex with other men while he watches or forcing her to watch while he has sex with other individuals. Women may be denied the ability to protect themselves from sexually transmitted diseases, including HIV, or unwanted pregnancy. Sexual abuse sends a powerful message that he not only controls her activities, he also controls her body.

Threats to Harm or Take
Children, Pets, or Property

Batterers may threaten to harm the children or pets in order to control the victim's behavior. This quote from Dr. G. L. Bundow * illustrates the point.

"Once when I tried to leave my ex-husband he took my dachshund puppy and threw him against the wall. He told me to remember those cries, because if I ever left him, those cries would haunt me, because they would be the cries of my young niece."

The victim may be told he will take everything she owns if she leaves him. The house is in his name, so is the checking account. Put yourself in the position of a victim for a minute. Think about leaving everything you own behind as you flee to a battered woman's shelter in the middle of the night. You have no money, no job, no car, perhaps no marketable skills. You have two small children who will need food, clothing, and shelter, and you are three months pregnant — the result of your partner's drunken rape. As bad as it is at home, you think, the alternative appears worse.

---

* G. L. Bundow, M.D., from the *JAMA Violence Compendium,* 1992.

Physical Abuse

Physical abuse ranges from pushing and shoving and slapping to biting, punching, kicking, throwing, choking, shooting, and stabbing. It also includes tying the woman down, restraining her, or leaving her in a dangerous place. Assaults involving weapons, especially firearms, may have deadly outcomes.

A mother of two children had been battered for many years. Her husband had recently been laid off and was drinking more than usual. One evening, after she returned from work, he suddenly grabbed a handgun, pointed it at her temple and pulled the trigger. But the gun jammed. He was so angry he threw down the gun and began pummeling her from head to toe with the only other weapon he had — his fists. She was able to escape. She had bruises from head to toe, but she was alive. Had the gun not jammed, she would have certainly been killed.

Physical assaults can be explosive and unexpected or methodically ruthless and unanticipated. They are also, unfortunately, repetitive in many instances. Of men who beat their wives, 47 percent do so three or more times a year.[*]

Although the pattern of injury has been described as being more likely to be of a central pattern — more injuries about the face and trunk than the extremities — any type of injury can be sustained.

---

[*] *Diagnostic and Treatment Guidelines on Domestic Violence.*
Los Angeles County Department of Children's Services.

Using Intimidation or Threats
of Physical Abuse

After the first episode of physical abuse, a batterer may not have to beat his partner to gain or maintain control. He only need to use the threat of violence — sometimes as subtle as giving her a certain look, using a gesture, or smashing something in a meaningful way. A woman who has been choked into unconsciousness in the past will certainly believe her batterer intends do it again when in the course of an argument he grabs their child's teddy bear and wrings its neck.

Chapter Five

HOW CAN WE INCREASE RECOGNITION OF DOMESTIC VIOLENCE?

Even though Chapters 2 and 3 list attributes often associated with victims and perpetrators, it is important to remember that *all* patients can be victims of domestic violence. No one is immune. There are however, some clues to the presence of domestic violence which can be ascertained from the history and physical examination.

Clues from the History

- The history of the incident is not consistent with the kind of injury.

A twenty-three-year-old woman comes to your office for evaluation of injuries that she says she sustained after falling down a flight of stairs. Her only injury is a black eye.

A fifty-year-old housewife says she accidentally slipped in the bathtub. She has bruises on both upper arms more suggestive of having been forcibly grabbed.

- There is a time delay between injuries and presentation. There are a variety of reasons why victims of domestic violence may not be able to seek medical attention for their injuries in a timely fashion — they may be afraid to leave the house while their partner is still in a rage, they may have no access to transportation, or they must conceal the fact that they sought medical care. Because of this, they may seek attention for injuries that are already beginning to heal.

Mary S. asked for an urgent appointment for evaluation of an injury to her left arm. On examination, you find bruises which are already turning green and yellow, suggestive of an injury at least three days old.

- The patient may have an "accident"-prone history.

A forty-nine-year-old housewife arrives at your clinic for evaluation of a "tension headache." A review of her chart reveals fourteen visits to the emergency department in the last two years. All of these visits were for minor injuries such as bruises and sprains due to "slips" and "falls."

- Suicide attempts or depression.

Your patient, Susan J., was brought to the Emergency Department by ambulance after ingesting forty aspirin tablets. When you ask her why she tried to kill herself she said she had a fight with her husband. Only after asking "what type of fight did you have?" did you learn her history of domestic violence.

- Repetitive psychosomatic complaints. These patients may have recurring physical complaints which are not suggestive of organic disease.

RECURRING PHYSICAL COMPLAINTS

Headaches	Numbness and tingling
Chest pains	Nervousness
Heart palpitations	Dyspareunia
Choking sensations	Pelvic pain

She may also be seen over and over again for any of a number of chronic pain syndromes, including chronic abdominal pain, chronic pelvic pain, or chronic headaches. Despite aggressive work-ups, no organic pathology is found.

On the other hand, the patient may present a picture of noncompliance with a medical regimen prescribed for a chronic condition — diabetes or hypertension. The real reason for not taking her medications may be that her partner is keeping them from her. She may miss appointments because she has no access to transportation and he refuses to take her, or he may cancel the appointments. One clinician describes "red-flagging" patients' charts when their male partner has called to cancel the appointment because in his practice this correlates with partner abuse.

The patient may complain of vague symptoms such as fatigue, lethargy, or listlessness. It may be very difficult to get her to articulate exactly what is bothering her. We may think of these individuals as difficult or problem patients. The reality is that these are patients with real, often life-threatening problems.

- She may have emotional complaints, including anxiety, panic attacks, sleep disorders, nervousness, depression, difficulty coping with parenting, or nonspecific complaints of marital problems, such as "things aren't going well at home" or "I am under a lot of stress at home recently."

- She may show signs and symptoms of alcoholism and drug abuse. Victims of domestic violence may turn to alcohol or drugs, including prescription sedatives and anxiolytics, as a way of coping with the violence.
- Beware of any injury during pregnancy. Abuse during pregnancy threatens not only the woman's health but also the outcome of the pregnancy. Battered women may experience "spontaneous" abortions, premature labor, low birthweight babies, and fetal injuries.
- Other pregnancy-related problems, such as substance abuse, poor nutrition, depression, and late or sporadic access to prenatal care, should also prompt direct inquiry about domestic violence. She may have a history of multiple abortions which he has forced her to have.
- Are there signs and symptoms of post-traumatic stress syndrome? Symptoms of increased arousal, sleep difficulties, irritability, difficulty concentrating, and hypervigilance are suggestive of post-traumatic stress syndrome. In addition, she may experience a numbing of general responsiveness, avoidance of stimuli associated with the trauma, or a persistent re-experiencing of the trauma, including recurrent dreams and flashbacks.

The Patient's Demeanor
Can Be a Clue

The patient may minimize the extent of the violence by her partner or seem inappropriately unconcerned about the nature or extent of her injuries. She may seem frightened, ashamed, evasive, or embarrassed. She may seem to be inappropriately emotional about minor injuries. She may close her eyes during much of the interview or assiduously avoid eye contact. She may be jumpy whenever the door is opened or fearful when someone enters the room.

The Companion's Behavior
Can Also Be a Clue

If the batterer has accompanied her for the medical visit, he may seem the picture of concern for his partner. He asks to stay with her during the entire visit, often holding her hand or hovering about her side. When you ask her a question, he gives the answer. She does not make an attempt to speak for herself. She may seem afraid or reluctant to disagree with his explanation of what has occurred.

Occasionally the batterer will display hostility or anger directed at her or at you during the visit. However, often, he will seem a loving husband, concerned only that his wife gets all the care she needs.

Asking Directly about
Domestic Violence

Because its presentation can be so varied, we may miss domestic violence if we rely only on clues to its presence.

Since every woman is a potential victim, in order to increase our recognition of domestic violence, we must ask directly if the woman is experiencing violence in her life. In order to do this you must:

- Ask the question in private. This means you must separate the patient from anyone who accompanied her. You must do this in a way that does not arouse suspicion and therefore protects her. Depending on the medical setting there are many ways to do this — you can ask the person to leave during the physical examination or you can send the patient to another area — such as the laboratory or x-ray department.
- Build trust with the patient by maintaining good eye contact, listening intently, and displaying empathetic concern.
- Remember that not all victims will respond to the same type of questioning. Try to vary your approach depending on the circumstances.

EXAMPLES OF QUESTIONS TO ASK WHEN YOU SUSPECT DOMESTIC VIOLENCE

"Mrs. Smith, many women experience some type of physical abuse in their lives. Has this ever happened to you?

"Sarah, whenever I see injuries of this type, it is often because someone hit them with a fist. Is that what happened to you?"

"You have a number of bruises. How did they happen?"

"Violence in the home is very common and can be very serious. Ms. Evans, I routinely ask all of my patients whether they are experiencing domestic violence because no one should have to live in fear and because there is help available."

"Relationships are sometimes violent. What happens when you fight in your home?"

"Ms. Smith, you seem frightened of your partner — has he ever hit you?"

"What happens when your spouse loses his temper?"

"Does your spouse use drugs or alcohol? (If so,) How does your spouse behave toward you when he is drinking or using drugs?"

"Hi Jane, how are things at home? How are things with you and Hank? All couples fight? Have you been having fights? How do you fight? Do you ever fight physically?"

If the patient gives a history of having had a spontaneous abortion, ask the question: "Was there a physical cause for your abortion?"

- If your method and manner of inquiry is working, keep using the same technique. If it is not working, try varying your approach.
- If your direct questions fail to confirm the existence of an abusive relationship, be sure to leave the door open by asking indirect questions.

"If you were experiencing violence in your home, would you know where to get help?"

Routine Screening

Because domestic violence is so prevalent and presents such a serious threat to the health and well-being of its victims, many experts are now recommending routine screening of all women for the existence of abuse in their lives. Questions about violence and other manifestations of partner abuse should be incorporated not only into the history of present illness, but also the social history, the past medical history, and the review of systems.

Questions about domestic violence should be incorporated in written health assessment tools used for new patients or for annual visits.

QUESTIONS THAT CAN BE INCORPORATED INTO A WRITTEN HEALTH ASSESSMENT

1. Are you in a relationship in which you have been physically hurt?

2. Have you ever been physically hurt in an intimate relationship?

3. Are you (have you ever been) in a relationship in which you felt you were treated badly? In what ways?

4. Has your partner ever harmed or threatened to harm someone or something you love?

5. Have you ever been forced to have sex when you did not want it? Have you ever been forced to participate in sexual practices which you didn't want to do?

It is important to develop a reminder system so that patients seen regularly will be queried about domestic violence on a periodic basis. In addition, women who do not admit to domestic violence on one visit may respond if asked on another visit. Red-flagging charts as reminders to ask about domestic violence on the next visit can be helpful.

The Family Violence Prevention Fund, a national organization, headquartered in San Francisco, has pioneered innovative responses to the epidemic of domestic violence. They are in the process of developing a screening tool which will be tested for effectiveness and eventually disseminated. For more information, contact their Resource Center at 1-800-313-1310.

Clues from the Physical Examination

Victims of domestic violence may try to hide injuries by wearing long sleeves or turtleneck garments. They may conceal black eyes with dark glasses or heavy make-up. Whenever possible you should have patients change from their street clothes into a hospital gown.

- Examine the entire body, noting areas of tenderness as well as areas with visible injuries.
- Injuries due to domestic violence may have a "central pattern," that is, injuries to the face, neck, throat, chest, breasts, abdomen, and genitals.
- Bear in mind that some injuries tend not to happen accidentally.

Accidental bumps to the head usually occur on the forehead or upper occipital area and not on the sides or directly on the top of the head.

Unintentional extremity bruises are usually seen on the outer part of the extremity; bruises on the inner aspect of the arms or thighs are strongly suggestive of *intentional* injury.

- Be suspicious of injuries suggestive of a defensive posture, such as bruises to the ulnar aspect of the forearm.
- As with child abuse, multiple injuries in various stages of healing suggest physical violence occurring over a period of time, most often in the setting of partner abuse.
- Any injury during pregnancy should be explored to determine if it was sustained as a result of domestic violence.
- In the very old, when the history is not forthcoming from the patient because of underlying dementia, examine the genital area for signs of hematomas, bleeding, or the insertion of foreign bodies.

Additional Sources of Information

Accompanying friends or family members may be able to give information about violence in the patient's relationship. Unless they volunteer the information, it will probably be necessary to confine the inquiry to questions of an indirect nature, such as, "How are things going for Mary at home?" or "Lila seems very sad, do you know why?" Questions that suggest you suspect or know of domestic violence could be construed as a violation of patient confidentiality, and in some circumstances could place her at risk of further violence (e.g., if the accompanying friend is also a confidant of the batterer).

Another valuable source of information is the patient's medical record. Charts that document repetitive use of emergency services (e.g. the accident-prone patient described previously) or extensive negative work-ups for functional complaints, such as chronic abdominal or pelvic pain, should prompt inquiry about domestic violence.

Ancillary laboratory tests are usually not helpful. The one exception is x-rays that show unsuspected old fractures, much as is the case in child abuse.

Chapter Six

WHAT TO DO WHEN SHE SAYS "YES" TO QUESTIONS ABOUT ABUSE

Once you have determined the presence of domestic violence, it is very important to assess, with the patient, the safety of her and her children.

Questions to Ask to Assure the Patient's Safety

Here are some questions to ask the patient that can be useful in assessing safety.

- Has the amount of physical violence increased in frequency and severity over the past year? How often does he attack/hit/or threaten you?
- Have you ever been hospitalized as a result of his abuse?

- Has he ever threatened you with a weapon? Has he ever used a weapon? Is there a gun in the house?
- Has he ever tried to choke you? Has he ever threatened to kill you? Have you ever been afraid you might die while he was attacking you?
- Does he use "upper drugs' such as amphetamines (speed), angel dust (PCP), cocaine, or crack cocaine?
- Does he get drunk every day or almost every day?
- Does he control your daily activities, such as where you can go, who you can be with, or how much money you can have?
- Were you ever beaten by him when you've been pregnant?
- Is he violent and constantly jealous of you? Has he ever said that if he can't have you, no one else can?
- Has he ever used threats or tried to commit suicide in order to get you to do what he wants?
- Have you ever threatened or attempted suicide because of problems in the relationship?
- Are you thinking of killing yourself now? Do you have a plan? A weapon?
- Is he violent toward your children?
- Is he violent outside of your home?

One of the most important questions you can ask is if *she* thinks it is safe to go home. She knows her situation better than anyone else. **The decision about going** home or not going home must ultimately be made by *her* and *respected* by you.

Published Tools

There are two published tools that can be of help when assessing danger. One is the *Physical Abuse Ranking Scale.** Any incident that is ranked higher than five or six on this scale indicates a high likelihood of extreme danger.

THE PHYSICAL ABUSE RANKING SCALE

1. Throwing things, punching the wall.

2. Pushing, shoving, grabbing, throwing things at the victim.

3. Slapping with an open hand.

4. Kicking, biting.

5. Hitting with closed fists.

6. Attempted strangulation.

7. Beating up (pinned to wall/floor, repeated kicks, punches).

8. Threatening with a weapon.

9. Assault with a weapon.

---

* PHYSICAL ABUSE RANKING SCALE from: "Identification and assessment, documentation and intervention." *Surgeon General's Workshop on Violence and Public Health Report.* October, 1985.

Another method of determining the amount of danger to your patient is a lethality checklist. One such scale has been published in a *Mile High United Way Special Report.*[*] This checklist consists of nineteen items. The higher the number of items checked, the greater the danger. Note however, that the absence of most of the items listed does not mean that danger does NOT exist.

THE LETHALITY CHECKLIST

1. Perpetrator objectifies partner (calls her names, body parts, animals, etc.).

2. Perpetrator blames victims for perceived injuries to herself.

3. Perpetrator is unwilling to turn victim loose.

4. Perpetrator is obsessed with victim.

5. Perpetrator is hostile/angry/furious.

6. Perpetrator appears distraught.

7. The relationship is extremely tense, volatile.

8. Perpetrator is extremely jealous, blaming the victim for all types of promiscuous behavior.

9. Perpetrator has perpetrated previous incidents of significant violence.

---

[*] LETHALITY CHECKLIST, Ibid.

10. Perpetrator has killed pets.

11. Perpetrator has made threats.

12. Perpetrator has made previous suicide attempts.

13. Perpetrator is threatening suicide.

14. Perpetrator has access to victim.

15. Perpetrator has access to guns.

16. Perpetrator uses alcohol.

17. Perpetrator uses amphetamines, speed, cocaine, crack, or other drugs.

18. Perpetrator has thoughts/ desires of hurting partner.

19. Perpetrator has no desire to stop violence/control behavior.

Use of these instruments to assess danger should never be a substitute for clinical judgment. Furthermore, even if the abusive situation ranks low on these scales, **if the patient feels she is in danger this should be the determining factor.**

Documentation
Careful attention to documentation in the medical record is very important in cases of abuse. If the patient chooses not to leave the relationship at this time, your record may be the only evidence of prior battering if she decides

to leave in the future. This is especially important if she seeks civil remedies such as divorce or child custody.

If she decides to leave, especially if she chooses to report the battery to the police, your records could be subpoenaed for court. The better the documentation of your medical records, including the legibility, the less likely you will actually have to take time out of your practice to appear in court.

The following are essential elements to be placed in the medical record:

ESSENTIAL ELEMENTS TO BE PLACED IN THE MEDICAL RECORD

History: Record a description of the abuse as she has described it to you. Use statements such as "the patient states she was beaten about the head by her husband using his fists." If she give you the specific name of the assailant, include it in your record — "she says her boyfriend John Smith struck her with a baseball bat last night."

Record all pertinent **physical findings**. Use a body map (see Appendix, p. 101) to supplement the written record. This is particularly important for injuries that manifest as tenderness without visible bruising.

Offer to **photograph** when the patient's injuries are visible. If the patient agrees, obtain permission in writing and attach to the chart. Polaroid photographs are especially useful in this situation as the adequacy of the photo can be ascertained before the patient leaves the medical setting. The name, date, time, medical record number, as well as your name and that of a witness to the photo, should be attached to the chart along with the photo. If standard film is used, be sure seal the film in an envelope with identifying data attached.

When serious injury or sexual abuse is detected, preserve all **physical evidence**. Torn or bloodstained clothing can be sealed in an envelope or bag. The same is true if a weapon is found during the examination.

If the patient does not confirm the abuse but **you are still suspicious** be sure to record this in the record. For example, "the patient tells me she fell down the stairs but her injuries are more compatible with a direct blow to the orbit."

Treatment

It is beyond the scope of this text to describe the treatment of injuries due to battering. However, it is very important to understand that "treatment" of victims of domestic violence is more than treating injuries or giving referral telephone numbers.

Many physicians feel frustrated in dealing with battered women because they believe the goal of any interaction is to get the woman to leave the relationship and go to a shelter as *a result of that visit*. However, that may not be what the woman wants or thinks is appropriate at that time. Physicians need to understand that leaving a batterer is not a single event, rather, it is a process which takes time — often years. You can help her get started or moved further along the road to leaving by giving her some very important messages, by providing her information about her options, and by letting her know that you are there to help and support her as she takes the steps necessary to free herself of the violence.

It is essential that physicians understand this process, respect the integrity of the victim, and support her efforts to make her own decision about what to do.

It is also important to understand that giving information about domestic violence to victims is, in fact, a therapeutic intervention.

"THERAPEUTIC" MESSAGES TO GIVE VICTIMS OF DOMESTIC VIOLENCE

- She needs to know she does not deserve to be battered — no matter what.
- She needs to know that battering is a common problem, affecting millions of women.
- She needs to know she is not alone and that help is available — from you and your staff as well as a host of resources in the community.
- She needs to know her options.

It is important to be very careful not to convey to the patient that she has failed you or disappointed you if she chooses not to leave the relationship at this time. Rather she needs to know that you understand the difficulties she faces, and you are prepared to support her in her actions and help her in whatever way you can.

Helping Her to Develop a Safety Plan

It is vital to assess the woman's safety and help her to develop a safety plan before she leaves the medical setting. If physician time is limited, the patient can be referred to another individual knowledgeable about domestic violence, such as a domestic violence advocate, a social worker, or a psychologist, to develop the safety plan.[*]

---

[*] Do not assume that all social workers or psychologists are trained in working with victims of domestic violence. It is essential you know the capabilities of your referral resources.

Questions to help assess and plan for safety:

1. Does she think it is safe to go home?
   - Where is her batterer now? Was he arrested? Was he arrested and released?
   - Does he have access to a firearm or other weapon?
   - Has he been threatening to kill her? Does she believe him?
   - Has he been harassing her or stalking her? Are his abusive behaviors escalating?

2. Does she have friends or family with whom she can stay?
   - Would she feel safe at their homes or is she afraid her batterer would come after her there?
   - Is she confident they would not inadvertently collude with the batterer by having him come get her, mistakenly thinking that they are helping to preserve the family or relationship?

3. Where are her children or other dependents? Does she think they are safe? Is she afraid they would be harmed if she didn't go home?

4. Does she want immediate access to a shelter or other temporary living situation?
   - If she doesn't want to go to a shelter now, be sure to give her the phone numbers in case she wants or needs to go at a later time.

- If she wants to go to a shelter, but there are no beds available what are her options? Motel vouchers? Admission to the hospital?

5. Does she need immediate medical or psychiatric intervention?
   - Is she suicidal?
   - Is she homicidal?
   - Does she need urgent crisis counseling to help her deal with the stress of the abuse?
   - If none of the above apply, be sure to give her telephone numbers to the domestic violence or crisis hotline in your community. And be sure to let her know how she can get in touch with you if she needs to.

6. If she wants to go home, be sure a definite follow-up appointment is scheduled and that she has information about community referrals (see below).

7. She should also be advised to have a safety plan in case she needs to leave home quickly. The following items should be hidden in a place she can access quickly in case of an emergency:
   - Identification for herself and her children (e.g. driver's license, passports, green cards, birth certificates)
   - Important documents (e.g. school and health records, insurance records, car titles, mortgage papers, marriage license, etc.)

- Copies of any protective orders, divorce or custody papers, or other court documents
- A small supply of any prescription medications or a list of the drugs and their doses
- Clothing, toys, and other comfort items for her and the children
- Extra set of car, house, and safety deposit box keys
- Phone numbers and addresses for family, friends, and community agencies

Referral

Appropriate referral depends on your knowing what services are available for battered women in your community. Many communities have a battered women's program with a shelter facility. The shelter may be a confidential shelter with the location known only to the staff of the program, or it may be a shelter where the address is common knowledge. You should know the capability of the shelter and alternatives for crisis housing if the shelter is full. Some communities have motel vouchers available through the police department or through social services or a charitable organization.

You should also know the services available through the battered women's program. Many offer advocates who help the victim wade through the legal system as she tries to obtain a restraining order or press charges. Most offer counseling, either one-on-one and/or group counseling. Counselors are often women who have survived the ordeal of domestic violence themselves. Battered women's shelters will often also assist residents of the shelter find permanent housing, employment, child care, and other essential services when they are ready to leave the shelter.

The programs may have twenty-four-hour hotlines in more than one language. Others have more limited hours. Almost all shelters have cards with information about their hotlines and other programs. You should obtain these cards and place them in strategic locations in you office or department.

Counseling

As mentioned above, many battered women's programs provide excellent counseling services. It may be necessary or appropriate in some instances to refer women to private counselors or to counselors affiliated with your institution. There are two caveats.

Couples counseling is, in most instances, contraindicated. It is usually impossible to get the batterer to accept and acknowledge his responsibility for the violence in the relationship. The abnormal power and control dynamics in the relationship make it impossible for her to be forthcoming in the sessions as well. She knows if she talks honestly about the violence, she faces retribution for the disclosure once she gets home.

The other *caveat* is to refer battered women only to counselors you know have expertise in the area of domestic violence. Counselors who don't understand the dynamics of domestic violence may give the victim the message that she is to blame for the abuse, rather than put the responsibility for the violence solely where it belongs — with the batterer. You can often obtain a list of skilled counselors from battered women's programs.

Social Services

In some practice settings, social services can be consulted early on to help with most of the referral process. Social workers trained in and knowledgeable about domestic violence may be able to work on the safety plan as well. It is very important that you discuss with the social worker exactly what needs to be done and check after the consultation to be sure it was done in a way that assured the victim's safety while still maintaining her integrity and authority over her own life.

Legal Services

If there is no battered women's program in your community or if they do not have legal services or referrals, you can give the woman the telephone number for the local legal-aid society or the local bar association. They may be able to help her find low-cost legal help.

Police

Battering is a crime in every state — however, it is frequently not reported to the police. There are many reasons for this. The woman may know from prior experience that the police response will not improve her safety and in some instances may actually increase the danger for her and her children. For example, if she calls the police to her home and their response is to simply walk the batterer around the block to "cool him off," she may be beaten severely after they leave. Even arrest may not be effective if the batterer is only locked up for a short period of time.

Other reasons why woman may not call the police:

- No access to a telephone.
- She thinks they won't believe her or won't take her seriously.
- She may have reason to fear police intervention because of something in her own history (e.g., undocumented resident status or a past criminal record).
- Her partner is the sole source of financial support for the family. She fears he may lose his job if he is arrested.
- She still loves him. She does not want him to go to jail. She just wants the violence to stop.
- She may have called them before (many times), but the response was not helpful (e.g. they did not come to the house or they came but believed his story that it was only a minor argument).

You should ask the woman if she wants to report the incident to the police or has already done so. If not, would she like you to call the police and have them come to your office or hospital to take the report? You should be familiar with the response of your community's police and district attorney to battering so that you can help the victim understand what to expect. Some police departments respond aggressively with same-day arrest. Others will merely take a telephone report. Some district attorneys' offices have a lackadaisical approach to domestic violence cases, others will pursue the case even if the victim has changed her mind about prosecution. A call to the local police department and district attorney's office can usually give you the information you need about the likely response.

Disposition

Only a small percentage of battered women require hospitalization for their injuries. Some require psychiatric hospitalization for suicidal, or more rarely, homicidal ideation. Most will be discharged from your care either to a shelter or to return home as dictated by the safety assessment and her desire. Before she leaves, set up a return visit or arrange a time when you can safely call her to check on how things are going.

Planning for Follow-up Care

Follow-up care is essential. As discussed earlier (see page 68), many battered patients will initially return to their batterer. It is very important to assess the situation on regularly scheduled return visits.

Chapter Seven

LEGAL ISSUES

Mandatory Reporting of Domestic Violence

Some states have enacted mandatory reporting of domestic violence. In some cases the report is to a social services agency, in others it is to the police. It is essential that the physician recognize that the act of reporting may increase risk to the patient in some circumstances. Batterers may have threatened their partners with further harm or death if they ever tell anyone about the violence. Reports made to police or other governmental agencies may result in someone from those institutions contacting the batterer. It may not necessarily result in him being removed from the home. Or if he is removed, it may be for a very short period. His discovery that she has told can precipitate an escalation of the violence.

Duty to Warn

Many states have laws requiring physicians to notify a third party if they have reason to believe their patient might harm that individual.

Liability for Reporting or Not Reporting

It is possible that a woman reported to be a victim of domestic violence may deny that this is the case and seek legal redress against the physician who reported her. It is important to be aware of legal liability protections if you live in a state with mandatory reporting. If the liability protections are not equivalent to those invoked with child abuse reporting, contact your state medical association's legal department to see if they can work to remedy the situation.

It is also possible that a battered woman or her family could seek legal redress against a physician who failed to identify and intervene in a case of domestic violence, especially if she later suffered severe injury or death. The good medical practice of routinely screening all women for domestic violence is an effective means of reducing this medicolegal risk.

Legal Options for the Patient

Criminal Actions

Battering is a crime in all fifty states. Criminal actions that can be taken against batterers include prosecution for assault, battery, aggravated assault or battery, harassment, intimidation, stalking, or attempted murder. The response of the police varies from jurisdiction to jurisdiction.

Civil Actions

Domestic violence victims may obtain either **temporary or permanent protective orders** which proscribe contact by the perpetrator with the victim, and sometimes the children and other family members. Community domestic violence agencies usually can help the victim deal with the process of obtaining the orders. It must be emphasized, however, that if a perpetrator is determined to harm the victim, the restraining orders may not offer any protection.

When the victim has decided to leave the relationship permanently she has the options of **legal separation and divorce.** If there are children, there will also be **child custody** issues to deal with.

Chapter Eight

PREPARING FOR AN OPTIMAL RESPONSE TO DOMESTIC VIOLENCE

An optimal medical response to domestic violence requires planning ahead. It also requires thought and preparation on many different levels, ranging from very personal to departmental or institutional and in most instances, includes community response as well.

Preparing Yourself

1. Become educated about the dynamics of domestic violence and about resources in your practice setting and community that are available to serve battered patients.
2. Examine your own attitudes about violence, especially violence directed toward women. Do you have some prejudices or

misunderstandings that might be playing a role in a failure to diagnose abuse in your patients? Have you been or are you currently in an abusive relationship? Have you been abusive or violent toward a current or former partner? Did you grow up in a violent home? Were you ever a victim of violence?

3. Honestly assess your own use and abuse of power, control, and violence in both your personal and your professional life. Think about how that abuse might affect your relationship with patients and staff.

4. Consider whether your behavior is giving messages to patients that you inadvertently collude with the abuser or blame the victim.

MESSAGES OF COLLUSION OR BLAME

- When we advise a victim to be more assertive or more accommodating to her partner as a way of stopping or avoiding the violence, we give the message that she is responsible, at least in part, for the abuse.

- When we fail to ask directly about domestic violence as a cause of a victim's injuries, we send a message of silent collusion with the perpetrator.

- When we fail to ask directly about domestic violence as a cause of a victim's injuries, we send a message of silent acceptance of the batterer's behavior.

---

5. Understand that leaving a battering relationship is a process which takes time (sometimes years). Despite your help, the woman may not leave, and in fact may suffer further injuries or illnesses due to her partner's abuse. Just as we persevere when trying to help patients stop smoking or change their diet, it is essential that we not become frustrated by slow progress and that we continue to support the woman as she struggles with leaving the abusive relationship.

Preparing Your Office or Department

1. Examine health-care policies and procedures in your practice setting to see if they are creating barriers that keep battered women from getting appropriate health care.

POLICIES THAT MAY
CREATE BARRIERS

- A policy of always allowing partners to be present during the history and physical examination makes it impossible to ask about abuse in the relationship.

- Public or semipublic screening of patients' chief complaints (e.g. at a triage desk where other individuals can see and hear the interaction) may lead to false reports of the cause of the injury. In busy clinics or emergency departments, this explanation may be accepted without question.

- Patient education or referral materials on domestic violence which are too large to easily hide may be left behind by patients afraid of retribution if their partner learns they have talked about the abuse.

---

2. Train all of your staff. The identification and proper referral of victims of domestic violence requires a team approach. Everyone on the team must understand the dynamics and dangers of domestic violence. Because of staff turnover as well as knowledge decay, this education must be repeated on a periodic basis. There are many resources available to help with physician and staff education.

RESOURCES FOR TRAINING
MEDICAL PERSONNEL

- Local battered women's programs usually have individuals who can come to your office or department for a training session on domestic violence. Remember their financial resources and time are usually limited. Reimburse them for time and travel if you can.

- Many state and local medical and specialty societies have materials on medical response to domestic violence.

- The American Medical Association has excellent materials on domestic violence as well as child abuse, child sexual assault, and elder abuse. They can be obtained by calling the AMA National Medical Resource Center — (312) 464-5066.

- Educational materials and background information on domestic violence can be obtained from The Family Violence Prevention Fund's Health Resource Center — (800) 313-1310.

3. Add new office or departmental policies and procedures that will increase the identification and appropriate referral of victims of domestic violence.

POLICIES THAT WILL INCREASE IDENTIFICATION AND REFERRAL OF VICTIMS OF DOMESTIC VIOLENCE

- Incorporate a variety of questions designed to detect violence in the home into written or verbal routine screening histories.

- Develop a reminder system, (e.g. a color-coded sticker) to place on charts of suspected victims of domestic violence. This will help remind you to ask about abuse during subsequent visits. Some clinicians place this type of sticker on charts of women whose partners call to cancel their scheduled appointments because of a high correlation in their practice with subsequent identification of domestic violence.

- Routinely make time available for a private interview whenever a partner accompanies the patient to the visit. This should be done in a manner that will not arouse suspicion on the part of the partner.

---

4. Let your patients know that you and your staff care about and are knowledgeable about domestic violence.

SOME WAYS TO LET YOUR PATIENTS KNOW YOU AND YOUR STAFF ARE KNOWLEDGEABLE AND CARE ABOUT DOMESTIC VIOLENCE

- **Place posters** in the waiting room which give information about domestic violence to patients as well as giving the message that they can talk to you and your staff about this issue. Some places to get posters include:

  AMA. Every physician who joins the AMA's National Coalition of Physicians Against Family Violence receives a poster to hang in the waiting room and a certificate to frame and place in the office. For information, call (312) 464-5066.

  Family Violence Prevention Fund. In 1994, the Fund initiated a public education campaign, "There Is No Excuse for Domestic Violence." Information about how to obtain materials from this campaign for your office or department can be obtained by calling the Fund at 1-800-313-1310.

  County and State Medical Associations and Specialty Societies. Many of these organizations have posters available for display in your practice setting.

  Local domestic violence shelters/programs may have posters with a general message about domestic violence as well as information about how to get access to their services.

- **Routinely ask** every patient you see about violence and abuse in their lives. This can be done in a nonthreatening manner by simply stating that you know domestic violence is very common so you are routinely asking every patient if they are involved in a violent relationship.

- **Speak and write** about domestic violence in your community. Let it be known that you are concerned about domestic violence and will marshal resources to help victims.

5. Develop protocols to guide your office or department staff on the optimal response to domestic violence. Protocols such as this are part of the 1994 Joint Commission for the Accreditation of Health Care Organizations (JCAHO) guidelines for both hospitals and ambulatory care settings. Based on a review of over a hundred written emergency department policies, a list of beneficial elements has been developed. All protocols should be hospital or clinic specific and should be widely disseminated to all staff.

However, it is important to remember that protocols alone are not enough to ensure that domestic violence is identified in the first place. One study found that there was no difference in the perception of battering as an important cause of women's injuries when emergency departments with and without protocols were compared.* Protocols must be accompanied by staff awareness and a commitment on the part of all providers to make domestic violence screening, treatment and referral a high priority in their practices.

---

* N.E. Isaac and R. L. Sanchez. "Emergency Department response to battered women in Massachusetts." *Annals of Emergency Medicine* 23:4. April 1994.

ELEMENTS TO INCLUDE IN WRITTEN PROTOCOLS FOR DOMESTIC VIOLENCE*

1. **Definitions** of domestic violence, including what types of behaviors and individuals are covered by the policies.

2. **Dynamics** of domestic violence. It is important to include a discussion of the abnormal power and control dynamics as well as a discussion of barriers to diagnosis, including the reasons why a patient may be reluctant to discuss the abuse.

3. **Indicators** or criteria for the identification of battered women and women at risk for battering, including presenting physical and psychological symptoms.

4. **Treatment** and specific interventions including referral numbers, discharge information and conveying the messages, such as "you are not alone" and "there is help available." Information on interviewing techniques, discharge and safety planning, and hospital procedures for taking photographs are also very helpful.

5. **State reporting requirements** should be specifically spelled out including a sample of the reporting form if available.

6. **Medical record documentation** is important, including use of a body map, photographs and details documenting the history and physical findings. Guidelines on what to do if abuse is suspected but not confirmed can be included here as well.

7. **Referrals.** The written policy and procedure should contain copies of referral materials including telephone numbers for battered women's shelters, programs, and social service and counseling agencies as well as legal

services and children's services. It is very important that these numbers are reviewed and updated on an annual basis.

8. A plan for ongoing **staff education** should be included in the policy.

*(Adapted from *Health Alert,* Volume 1, Number 1. A publication of the Family Violence Prevention Fund in collaboration with the Pennsylvania Coalition Against Domestic Violence.)

6. Provide information on domestic violence and community resources that patients can take with them. These materials must contain accurate information and be small enough to be concealed in a purse or shoe. Cards such as the one shown here can be placed in the examining room, women's rest room or other places in which victims could pick them up in private.

"SAFE CHOICES"

"SAFE CHOICES" for domestic violence victims

DOMESTIC VIOLENCE CRISIS LINE
1-800-TRY-NOVA
(1-800-879-6682)

LOCAL REFERRAL _____
OR TALK TO YOUR DOCTOR

Crisis Line provided by National Association of Victims' Assistance (NOVA)
Distributed by California Medical Association Alliance

In 1995 there is expected to be funding for a national domestic violence hotline. Check with 800 information (1-800-555-1212) for this number.

7. Establish a follow-up process once domestic violence has been identified. Too often, victims of domestic violence are referred out of the health-care system — to shelters or counseling — and the abuse is never addressed by the health-care practitioner again. Because a woman may make many attempts before she is finally successful in leaving a violent relationship, a simple referral may not result in a change in her situation, just as a single referral to a "Stop Smoking" program may not result in smoking cessation. Practitioners with ongoing relationships with their patients must routinely and repeatedly discuss the possibility of domestic violence in their patients' lives.

Improving Awareness of Community Services

Women in abusive relationships need services beyond those traditionally provided in the medical setting. Therefore, you need to be aware of the availability of such services in the community.

1. Develop lists, with phone numbers, for battered women's shelters, safe houses, and other resources as well as for programs for batterers. Update the lists at least annually. Remember, domestic violence shelters and hotlines may close due to inadequate funding. Imagine giving a woman in danger a phone number no longer in service!
2. Be familiar with the capacities of local facilities and services, including the number of beds,

intake procedures (most programs want to talk directly to a woman before admittance), and entrance requirements at local shelters. Some battered women's shelters preferentially take in women with children. They may not be viewed as hospitable or acceptable places by elderly victims or victims of lesbian abuse. There are practically no shelters for male victims of domestic violence. The best way for you to become knowledgeable about the shelter services in your community is to meet regularly with their staff.

3. Learn about policies related to alcohol and drug abuse. Some shelters will not house women acutely intoxicated or under the influence of street drugs. It may be necessary to refer such patients to alcohol or drug abuse programs before or concurrent with referral to the shelter. Never assume, however, that treatment for substance abuse alone is an effective intervention for victims or perpetrators of violence.

4. Know the alternatives when shelters are not available or not appropriate for a given individual. In some communities, charitable organizations make motel vouchers available for temporarily housing people in need.

Preparing Your Hospital, Academic Medical Center, or Multi-physician Group Practice

In the hospital, academic, or group practice setting, establishment of an interdepartmental domestic violence committee can greatly improve medical response to domestic violence. DV committees should include physician and nursing representatives from the various medical and surgical specialties, as well as from support services. Community representation can greatly enhance the effectiveness of the committee. If time and resources do not permit regular representation by certain community officials, such as prosecutors or law enforcement, it is very important to have them attend as invited guests so that they can both give information about their attitudes and approach to domestic violence and so they can learn what you are doing in your health-care setting.

If possible, the committee should be set up to assure that minutes of the committee cannot be used by the legal system. In that way, issues requiring patient confidentiality can be discussed without endangering or harming the victim-patient.

Domestic violence committees can be used for the following purposes:

1. An ongoing education vehicle for members of the committee. By having representatives from the police, legal community, shelter community, and survivors of domestic violence participate, physicians and other hospital staff

can increase their knowledge about all aspects of domestic violence.

2. Because the members of the committee will, in general, be more knowledgeable about domestic violence, they can serve as a resource for the rest of the hospital or clinic staff.

3. The committee can be responsible for the development of written policies, procedures, and referral lists for the hospital or group practice. They can also be sure that materials are periodically updated. In addition, because it includes representatives or guests from community agencies, the committee is in a position to assess the adequacy and limitations of resources to meet the needs of victims.

4. The committee can be responsible for formal ongoing education of the hospital or group practice by arranging grand rounds, guest lectures, and teleconferences on aspects of domestic violence.

5. Interdisciplinary patient management. If the committee's proceedings are protected from discovery, the committee can play a very valuable role in assuring a coordinated response to victim's needs.

EXAMPLE OF
INTERDISCIPLINARY
PATIENT MANAGEMENT

Susan M. was a battered woman for ten years. Her husband, an attorney of some stature in the community, was her batterer. He was also an alcoholic. He insisted she drink with him and had beaten her on several occasions when she had tried to quit drinking. He frequently told her no one would believe her if she talked about the violence, because after all he was an attorney and she was "just a drunk." After a particularly brutal beating, Susan went to her local emergency department for evaluation and treatment of her injuries. There for the first time she talked about the abuse.

The emergency physician consulted both psychiatry (the designated referral for her hospital) and the alcohol counselor. At the patient's request the police were called. The husband was arrested and charged with battery. The patient was referred to the battered women's shelter for individual and group counseling.

Over the ensuing months, the patient returned to the relationship several times and continued to struggle with alcohol abuse. She intermittently contacted various members of the domestic violence team — the psychiatrist, the alcohol counselor, and the shelter counselor. The members of the team were able to develop a coordinated response for her, giving a consistent message of support and offers of ready availability of services.

Susan was eventually able to stop drinking and permanently leave the violent relationship.

SUGGESTED REPRESENTATIVES FOR A HOSPITAL OR GROUP PRACTICE DOMESTIC VIOLENCE COMMITTEE

Physician representatives
Internal Medicine
Family Practice
Ob/Gyn
Emergency Medicine
General Surgery
Surgical Subspecialties (especially ENT, Ophthalmology, Maxillofacial, and Plastics)
Orthopedics
Pediatrics
Psychiatry

Nursing representatives
In-house Nursing Supervisor
Emergency Department Nurse Manager
Nurse practitioners in Family Practice, OB-Gyn, Pediatrics

Support services representatives
Social services
Alcohol and drug abuse services
Employee assistance personnel
Clergy
Security

Community representatives
Shelter directors/ counselors
Legal services for battered women
Clergy
Police
District Attorneys
Victims/survivors

Working with Your Community

There is a great variability in community awareness and response to domestic violence. Physicians have a responsibility, as does every other community member, to work to improve the overall health of their community.

There are a number of ways that physicians can do this in the area of domestic violence.

SUGGESTED WAYS FOR PHYSICIANS TO IMPROVE THE RESPONSE OF THEIR COMMUNITY TO DOMESTIC VIOLENCE

- Give lectures on domestic violence to local community groups, such as the Rotary Club, the PTA, or women's clubs.

- Write articles about domestic violence for the local newspapers. Be sure to include information, including phone numbers, on local shelters and domestic violence programs.

- Support local domestic violence shelters and programs — volunteer to work, hold a fund-raiser, or write a check.

- Form a community coordinating council on domestic violence. Such councils typically include representatives from local government, domestic violence programs, the police and legal communities, as well as survivors of domestic violence. If your community forms a council, make sure the medical community is represented.

Other Contributions You Can Make

There are many other ways in which you as a physician can become involved in the prevention of, and early intervention in, domestic violence.

1. Involve yourself in organized medicine, and work to ensure that domestic violence is added to the agenda of your medical or specialty society. Resolutions adopted at the annual meetings of state and national medical associations can become policies that direct the governmental and educational efforts of that association.

2. Work with state and federal legislators and domestic violence advocates and experts toward meaningful legislation aimed at decreasing domestic violence and increasing the services available for victims. Physician input can help avoid legislation that may have inadvertent negative consequences for victims.

WORKING WITH LEGISLATORS

A state legislator crafted a bill to require the mandatory reporting of injuries due to domestic violence. Because of efforts by prosecutors, the bill initially included language that would have made it a misdemeanor if physicians failed to document certain aspects of the case in the medical record. Activist physicians were able to convince the legislator that this would be apt to discourage, rather than encourage, physicians to ask about abuse — even though accurate documentation of abuse is very important, The language on documentation was changed from a mandate to a recommendation.

---

3. Network with other medical people and advocates in the field of domestic violence to find meaningful ways to make a difference in domestic violence prevention and early intervention. We formed Physicians for a Violence-free Society[*] to provide this type of opportunity. We hope you will join us.

---

[*] Physicians for a Violence-Free Society, 5323 Harry Hines Blvd., Dallas, Texas, 75235-8579. Telephone (214) 559-8807.

APPENDIX A
INJURY LOCATION CHART

Indicate, with arrow from description to body, where injury was observed. Indicate number of injuries of each type in space provided.

ENCOUNTERS:

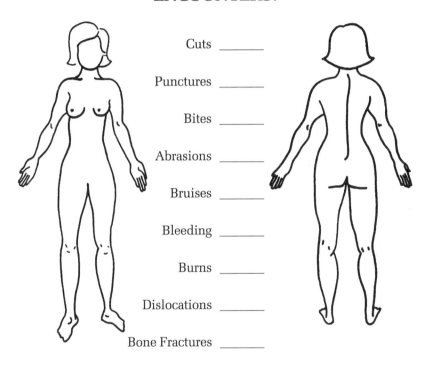

Cuts _____

Punctures _____

Bites _____

Abrasions _____

Bruises _____

Bleeding _____

Burns _____

Dislocations _____

Bone Fractures _____

Mark and describe all bruises, scratches, lacerations, bite marks, etc.

APPENDIX B
EXAMPLE OF A DOMESTIC
VIOLENCE PROTOCOL

PURPOSE: It is the policy of this department to provide a safe and secure environment for all patients brought to this facility. This policy will provide general guidelines for responding to specific needs identified by Emergency Department staff in dealing with domestic violence victims brought to the Department of Emergency Medicine.

PROCEDURE: (If Emergency Department staff notifies the Security Department)

1. It is the responsibility of the Security Department staff to provide a safe environment for all victims of domestic violence.
2. If upon receiving information from the Emergency Department staff that a person is identified as a victim of domestic violence, immediately notify Security supervisor at (extension). Do not use radios unless it is an emergency.
3. All information is to be kept confidential.
4. If necessary, restrict or monitor visitation to patient/victim when identified — keep parties separate.
5. Restrain or escort the perpetrator from the hospital premises.
6. Notify the local Police if needed to ensure safety of the victim, family or staff and to remove the actor if necessary.

7. If the victim has a PFA against the actor, this can be verified by calling Coordinator for PFA papers — Family Division at 555-5555. The final PFA papers are also on a computer at the Sheriff's office. This can be accessed by calling 555-5555. We have made arrangements to get the condition of the order by calling them. (Pay attention to the order, i.e., visitation rights, etc.)

NOTE: If we note suspicious behavior that may indicate domestic violence is involved. i.e., man hovering over or restraining a female patient, verbal or physical abusive behavior, etc., inform the Emergency Department staff of what you observed.

8. If the victim cannot gain access to a women's shelter for the night, they may be referred to the Mercy Health Center. Specific apartments have been set up to accommodate them. We may even escort victims over there. At no time will we release information about their location to anyone outside the Emergency Department staff, Social Services staff or the Domestic Violence Advocate at Mercy Hospital.

9. This protocol will be reviewed yearly at staff meeting and updated as needed.

APPENDIX C
DOMESTIC SAFETY ASSESSMENT

Over the past several years, domestic violence has come to be recognized as an important, often overlooked, health issue in our society. The Mercy Hospital of Pittsburgh's mission is to care for our patients who are in need. **We would like to help you identify whether you are a victim of abuse or neglect. To receive help is *your* decision — let us know if you have questions or would like to discuss your situation further.** Following are some questions to help you and us evaluate if you are in an abusive situation. Please respond to them openly.

This information is part of your healthcare record. Your responses will not be released to anyone without your written consent, except as otherwise provided by law. If you do not feel comfortable talking today, you can call us at (extension).

1. Do you feel safe at home?   ☐ Yes ☐ No
   If no, why do you feel this way?

   _____
   _____
   _____

2. We all have disagreements — when
   you and your partner or a family
   member argue, have you ever been
   physically hurt or threatened?   ☐ Yes ☐ No

3. Do you feel your partner or a
   family member controls (or tries to
   control) your behavior too much?   ☐ Yes ☐ No

4. Does he/she threaten you?   ☐ Yes ☐ No

5. Has your partner (or other family
   member) ever hit, pushed, shoved,
   punched or kicked you?   ☐ Yes ☐ No

6. Have you ever felt forced to engage
   in unwanted sexual acts/contact
   with your partner or other family
   member?   ☐ Yes ☐ No

If there are problems, we would like to help — please
let us know.

1. Would you like to discuss your
   situation?   ☐ Yes ☐ No

2. Would you like additional
   information on Domestic Violence?   ☐ Yes ☐ No

3. Declined referral.   ☐ Yes

SELECTED READING LIST

Items marked with an asterisk are recommended for your patients.

Allen, R.L. and Kivel, P. "Men changing men." *Ms. Magazine* 5(2):50. 1994.

Ammerman, R.T. and Hersen, M. *Assessment of Family Violence: a Clinical and Legal Sourcebook.* Wiley. 1992.

Arias, I. and Pape, K.T. "Physical abuse." in L. L'Abate, Ed., *Handbook of Developmental Family Psychology and Psychopathology,* 284-308. New York: Wiley. 1994.

Astor, R.A. "Children's moral reasoning about family and peer violence: the role of provocation and retribution." *Child Development* 65(4):1054. 1994.

Bachman, R. *Violence Against Women: a National Crime Victimization Survey Report.* Washington, D.C.: United States Department of Justice, Justice Statistics. 1994.

Bean, C.A. *Women Murdered by the Men They Loved.* Binghamton, NY.: Haworth Press. 1992.

Bell, C.C., Jenkins, E.J., Kpo, W., and Rhodes, H. "Response of emergency rooms to victims of interpersonal violence." *Hospital and Community Psychiatry* 45(2):142-6. 1994.

Berenson, A.B., Wiemann, C.M., Wilkinson, G.S., Jones, W.A., and Anderson, G.D. "Perinatal morbidity associated with violence experienced by pregnant women." *Am. J. of Obstetrics and Gynecology* 170(6):1760-6, discussion 1766-9. 1994.

Berrios, D.C. and Grady, D. "Domestic violence: risk factors and outcomes." *West. J. Med.* 155:133-5. 1991.

Brainerd, W.T. *Medical Psychology of Spouse Abuse. Index of New Information with Authors and Subjects.* Washington, D.C.: Abbe Pubs. Assn. 1993.

Brandt, E.N. Jr. "The unspoken chief complaint: family violence." *J. Oklahoma State Med. Assn.* 87(4):178-80. 1994.

Bray, R.L. "Remember the children." *Ms. Magazine* 5(2):38. 1994.

* Browne, A. *When Battered Women Kill.* New York: Macmillan/Free Press. 1987.

———— "Violence against women: relevance for medical practitioners." *JAMA* 267:3184-3189. 1992.

Burns, B. "Families in pain." *North Carolina Medical J.* 55(4):127-9. 1994.

Cantos, A.L., Neidig, P.H., and O'Leary, K.D. "Injuries of women and men in a treatment program for domestic violence." *J. Family Violence* 9(2):113. 1994.

Chambliss, L. "All in the family." *J. Emerg. Med. Services* 23(4):34-8, 41, 43-4. 1994.

Chez, N. "Helping the victim of domestic violence." *Am. J. Nursing* 94(7):32. 1994.

"Controlling violence at home." *University of California Berkeley Wellness Letter* 10(7):7. 1994.

Dannenberg, A.L., Baker, S.P., and Li, G. "Intentional and unintentional injuries in women. An overview." *Annals of Epidemiology* 4(2):133-9. 1994.

Diagnostic and Treatment Guidelines on Domestic Violence. Chicago: American Medical Association. 1992.

Flitcraft, A. "Physicians and domestic violence: challenges for prevention." *Health Affairs* 12(4):154-61. 1993.

Geller, J.A. *Breaking Destructive Patterns: Multiple Strategies for Treating Partner Abuse.* Free Press: New York. 1992.

Gelles, R. and Loseki, D. (Eds.). *Current Controversies on Family Violence.* Newbury Park, California: Sage. 1993.

Goldberg, W. G. and Tomlanovich, M.C. "Domestic violence victims in the emergency department: new findings." *JAMA* 251:3259-3264. 1984.

Grunfeld, A.F., Ritmiller, S., Mackay, K., Cowan, L., and Hotch, D. "Detecting domestic violence against women in the emergency department: a nursing triage model." *J. Emergency Nursing* 20(4):271-4. 1994.

Haugaard, J.J. "Sexual abuse in families." in L. L'Abate, Ed., *Handbook of Developmental Family Psychology and Psychopathology,* 309-329. New York: Wiley. 1994.

Hirshman, L. "Making safety a civil right." *Ms. Magazine* 5(2):44. 1994.

Hoff, L. A. *Battered Women as Survivors.* New York: Routledge. 1990.

Holtzworth-Munroe, A. and Stuart, G.L. "The relationship standards and assumptions of violent versus nonviolent husbands." *Cognitive Therapy and Research* 18(2):87-103. 1994.

Ingrassia, M., Beck, M., and Cowley, G. "Patterns of abuse." *Newsweek* 124(1):26. 1994.

Isaac, N.E. and Sanchez, R.L. "Emergency department response to battered women in Massachusetts." *Annals of Emergency Medicine* 23(4):855-8. 1994.

* Island, D. and Letellier P. *Men Who Beat the Men Who Love Them: Battered Gay Men and Domestic Violence.* Binghamton, NY: Haworth Press. 1991.

* Jones, A. *Next Time, She'll Be Dead: Battering and How to Stop It.* Boston: Beacon Press. 1994.

Kashani, J.H., Daniel, A.E., and Dandoy, A.C. "Family violence: impact on children." *J. Am. Acad. Child Adolescent Psychiatry* 31(2):181-189. 1992.

* Kilgore, N.. *Every Eighteen Seconds: A Journey through Domestic Violence.* Volcano, California: Volcano Press. 1993.

————— *Sourcebook for Working with Battered Women.* Volcano, California: Volcano Press. 1993.

* Klinect, P.L. *Beaten, Bruised, and Abandoned: the Unbelievable Story of an Abused Wife.* El Cajon, California: Tom-N-Pam. 1994.

* Kress, P.A. "Living with the enemy." (Bibliography on domestic violence.) *Library Journal* 119(13):106. 1994.

* Langan, P.A., and Innes, C.A. *Preventing Domestic Violence Against Women.* Washington, DC: U.S. Dept. of Justice, Bureau of Justice Statistics. 1986.

Leidig, M.W. "The continuum of violence against women: psychological and physical consequences." *J. Am. College Health* 40(4):149-155. 1992.

Lipsyte, R. "O.J. syndrome." *Am. Health* 13(7):50. 1994.

Loring, M.T., et al. "Health care barriers and interventions for battered women." *Public Health Reports* 109(3):328-38. 1994.

Malloch, M.S. and Webb, S.A. "Intervening with male batterers: a study of social workers' perceptions of domestic violence." *Social Work and Social Sciences Review* 4(2):119-147. 1993.

Marecek, Mary. *Breaking Free from Partner Abuse: Voices of Battered Women Caught in the Cycle of Domestic Violence.* Buena Park, California: Morning Glory Press. 1993.

Marano, H. "Inside the heart of marital violence." *Psychology Today* 26:48-53. 1993.

Marr, J. "The epidemic of violence. Physicians can play a key role in helping stop domestic violence." *Michigan Medicine* 93(5):34-49. 1994.

* Martin, Del. *Battered Wives.* Volcano, California: Volcano Press. 1981. (Revised Ed.)

Marwick, C. "Health and justice professionals set goals to lessen domestic violence." *JAMA* 271(15):1147-8. 1994.

McLeer, S.V. and Anwar, R.A. "The role of the emergency physician in the prevention of domestic violence." *Annals of Emergency Medicine* 16:1155-1161. 1987.

Meoli, M. "Helping the battered woman help herself." *J. Emerg. Med. Services: JEMS* (19(2):116. 1994.

* NiCarthy, Ginny. *Getting Free: You Can End Abuse and Take Back Your Life.* Seattle: The Seal Press. 1986, 1990.

* Nordquist, J. *Violence Against Women: a Bibliography.* Santa Cruz, California: Reference and Research Services. 1992.

Novello, A.C., Rosenberg, M., and Saltzman, L. "From the Surgeon General, U.S. Public Health Service." *JAMA* 267:3132. 1992.

Prince, J.E. and Arias, I. "The role of perceived control and the desirability of control among abusive and nonabusive husbands." *Am. J. Family Therapy* 22(2):126. 1994.

Randall, T. "Domestic violence intervention calls for more than treating injuries." *JAMA* 264:939-940. 1990.

———— "Domestic violence begets other problems of which physicians must be aware to be effective." *Ibid.* 943-944. 1990.

————— "Tools available for health care providers whose patients are at risk for domestic violence." *JAMA* 266(9):1179. 1991.

* Randolph, L.B. "Battered women: how to get and give help." *Ebony* 49(11): 112. 1994.

Renzetti, C.M. *Violent Betrayal: Partner Abuse in Lesbian Relationships.* Newbury Park, California: Sage. 1992.

Roberts, J.F. "One hospital's response to the fight against domestic violence." *J. Healthcare Protection Management* 10(1):27-32. Winter, 1993-94.

Salber, P.S. "Improving emergency department response to victims of domestic violence." *Western J. Medicine* 159(5):599-600. 1993.

Schiavone, F.M., et al. "Hitting close to home. Domestic violence and the EMS responder." *J. Emerg. Med. Services: JEMS* 19(2):112-5, 118-21, 123. 1994.

Serra, P. "Physical violence in the couple relationship: a contribution toward the analysis of the context." *Family Process* 32(1):21-33. 1993.

Shalala, D.E. "Domestic terrorism: an unacknowledged epidemic." (Transcript of a speech by the Secretary of Health and Human Services.) *Vital Speeches* 60(15):450. 1994.

Shepherd, J. (Ed.). *Violence in Health Care: a Practical Guide for Coping with Violence and Caring for Victims.* New York: Oxford University Press. 1994.

Smilkstein, G., et al. "Conjugal conflict and violence: a review and theoretical paradigm." *Family Medicine* 26(2):111-6. 1994.

Smith Fliesher, S. *Closeted Screams: A Service Provider Handbook for Same-Sex Domestic Violence Issues.* Aurora, Colorado: Soria Smith Fliesher. 1992.

Smolowe, J. "When violence hits home." *Time* 144(1):18. 1994.

Snyder, J.A. "Emergency department protocols for domestic violence." *J. Emergency Nursing* 20(1):65-8. 1994.

Sonkin, D. J. *Stopping Domestic Violence: A Counselor's Guide to Learning to Live without Violence.* Volcano, California: Volcano Press. 1995.

* Sonkin, D.J. and Durphy, M. *Learning to Live without Violence: A Handbook for Men.* Volcano, California: Volcano Press. 1989. (Third Edition.)

* ———— and ———— . *Aprender a Vivir Sin Violencia.* (Spanish edition of *Learning to Live without Violence*). Volcano, California: Volcano Press. 1995.

Spaccarelli, S., Sandler, I.N., and Roosa, M. "History of spouse violence against mother: correlated risks and unique effects in child mental health." *J. Family Violence* 9(1):79-98. 1994.

Stacey, W.A., et al. *The Violent Couple.* Westport, Connecticut: Greenwood. 1994.

* Stark, E. and Flitcraft, A. "Spouse abuse." in *Violence in America: a Public Health Approach.* New York: Oxford University Press. 1991.

* Statman, J.B. *The Battered Woman's Survival Guide: Breaking the Cycle.* Dallas, Texas: Taylor Publishing Company. 1990.

Streisand, B. and Goode, E. "Till death do them part?" *U.S. News and World Report* 117(1):24. 1994.

Sugg, N.K. and Inui, T. "Primary care physicians' response to domestic violence: opening Pandora's box." *JAMA* 267:3157-3160. 1992.

Swisher, K. L., Wekesseer, C., and Barbour, W. (Eds.), *Violence Against Women.* San Diego, California: Greenhaven Press. 1994.

Taylor, W.K. and Campbell, J.C. "Treatment protocols for battered women." *Response* 14:16-21. 1992.

Tilden, V.P. and Shepherd, P. "Increasing the rate of identification of battered women in an emergency department: use of a nursing protocol." R*esearch in Nursing and Health* 10:209-215. 1987.

Tilden, V.P., et al. "Factors that influence clinicians' assessment and management of family violence." A*m. J. Public Health* 84(4):628-33. 1994.

"Too much of it around: domestic violence." *Economist* 332(7872):A25. 1994.

Turk, M. "Striking back." *Am. Health* 13(7):44. 1994.

Walker, Lenore E. *The Battered Woman.* New York: Harper and Row. 1979.

"What's love got to do with it?" *Ms. Magazine* 5(2):34. 1994.

* Zambrano, M.M. *Mejor Sola que Mal Acompanada: Para la Mujer Golpeada — for the Latina in an Abusive Relationship.* Spanish and English. Seattle: Seal Press Feminist. 1985.

Order Form

_____ **The Physician's Guide to Domestic Violence:** *How to ask* $10.95
the right questions and recognize abuse . . . another way to save a life
by Patricia R. Salber, M.D., and Ellen Taliaferro, M.D.

_____ **Learning to Live without Violence:** *A Handbook for Men* $13.95
by Daniel Jay Sonkin, Ph.D. and Michael Durphy, M.D.

_____ **Aprender a Vivir Sin Violencia.** Spanish edition of *Learning* $13.95
to Live Without Violence

_____ **Learning to Live without Violence:** *Worktape* $15.95
(2 C-60 cassettes)

_____ **Stopping Domestic Violence:** *A Counselor's Guide to* $29.95
Learning to Live Without Violence by Daniel Jay Sonkin,
Ph.D., hardcover

_____ **Every Eighteen Seconds:** *A Journey Through Domestic* $8.95
Violence by Nancy Kilgore

_____ **Sourcebook for Working with Battered Women** $17.95
by Nancy Kilgore

_____ **Battered Wives** by Del Martin $12.95

_____ **Conspiracy of Silence:** *The Trauma of Incest* $12.95
by Sandra Butler

_____ **Menopause, Naturally:** *Preparing for the Second Half of Life,* $13.95
Updated, by Sadja Greenwood, M.D., M.P.H.

_____ **Menopausia Sin Ansiedad.** Spanish edition of $13.95
Menopause, Naturally

_____ **Period.** by JoAnn Gardner-Loulan, Bonnie Lopez and $9.95
Marcia Quackenbush

_____ **La Menstruacion.** Spanish edition of *Period.* $9.95

_____ **Goddesses** by Mayumi Oda $14.95

_____ **Lesbian/Woman** by Del Martin and Phyllis Lyon, hardcover $25.00

(continued on next page)

Youth and other titles from Volcano Press

To order directly, please send check or money order for the price of
the book(s) plus $4.50 shipping and handling for the first book, and
$1.00 for each additional book to Volcano Press, P.O. Box 270 ER,
Volcano, CA 95689. Order by phone with a VISA or MasterCard by
calling toll-free, 1-800-VPWYMEN (1-800-879-9636).

California residents please add appropriate sales tax.

Volcano Press books are available at quantity discounts for bulk
purchases, professional counseling, educational, fund-raising or pre-
mium use. Please call or write for details.

☐ Please send a free catalog to:

Name: _____

Address: _____

City, State, Zip: _____